RECOVERING FAITH

Volume 1

RECOVERING FAITH

WORDS FOR THE WAY

Volume 1

A Collaborative Project Between

The National Association for
Christian Recovery &
The Work of the People

edited by Kelly Hall

Vision statement: To provide faith-based communities a process of transformational recovery to aid people suffering with addiction, trauma, and abuse.

Mission statement: We are passionate about providing resources and training for faith-based communities so those in need of transformational recovery from addiction, abuse, and trauma can find it within their community. We provide the following:

- Consulting services

- Education and educational resources

- Best Practices

- Research and development

ISBN-13: 978-1508818847

ISBN-10: 1508818843

Published in association with Samizdat Creative, a division of Samizdat Publishing Group, LLC (samizdatcreative.com).

Contents

Powerlessness

CURRICULUM

KIM V. ENGELMANN

"I begged the Lord three times to liberate me *from its anguish*; and *finally* He said to me, 'My grace is enough to cover and sustain you. My power is made perfect in weakness.' *So ask me about my thorn*, inquire about my weaknesses, and I will gladly go on and on—*I would rather stake my claim in these* and have the power of the Anointed One at home within me. I am at peace and even take pleasure in any weaknesses, insults, hardships, persecutions, and afflictions for the sake of the Anointed because when I am at my weakest, He makes me strong."

—*2 Corinthians 12:8-10,* The Voice

DEVOTIONAL REFLECTIONS

The process of recovery is learning to actually boast about my own inabilities, my failures, my shortcomings, and ultimately my own powerlessness. What does it mean to boast in these inadequacies? I think it boils down to recognizing the truth of my desperate weakness, and once realized, I will then be astoundingly grateful and eagerly dependent upon God's initiative in my life. I will declare boldly that Christ alone is my strength and my song!

The catch is that God seems to be a great respecter of people's choices. As long as I hold onto what I mistakenly think I can handle on my own, as long as I believe that I have the power to change by myself, God will allow me to run with that choice. I usually don't hear people talk about how "delighted" they are by the fact that they are weak and have hardships and difficulties. It seems that Paul's delight in all this comes from his profound love for Jesus, and his deep desire that Jesus be glorified in Paul's own powerlessness. It's as if he is saying, "I blew it, but this is a great opportunity for You now, Lord! Take over . . . here's Your chance . . . cause right now I know I can't." What a statement of powerlessness from someone who had wielded such tyrannical power over Christians, even sending them to their death! Of course the paradox is always present. Look at the power these words of Scripture have for us today.

QUESTIONS FOR REFLECTION

How did Jesus teach us about powerlessness? How did He demonstrate it in His own life?

Why is it difficult for us to "delight" in our weakness and powerlessness? What forces in our culture pull us away from dependency on God?

What needs to happen for us to see "the light" of our own powerlessness?

The paradox is, of course, that when we surrender and recognize our powerlessness we become scooped up by a great and powerful God who then empowers us by His grace.

How would you describe God's power at work in us, as different from the power of the world?

In the film, there was mention of God paying attention when people come to the end of their own resources. In what way is this humorous? Tragic? Hopeful? What does this say about the heart of God?

PRAYER

Lord, have mercy on my desire to be self-sufficient and master of my own destiny. What a lonely road, and how powerless I am to add even an inch to my height! Again and again, I am deluded into believing that I can do life without You. Forgive me, and scoop me up. Help me to know that You love me just as I am, with all of my weakness. Shine through those weaknesses, because they are thin and fragile places in me that will let others see You more clearly.

I throw myself on Your grace, in utter dependence and with wild gratitude. You are my life, and I cling to You. In Jesus's name. Amen.

WRITE YOUR OWN PRAYER

A BLESSING FOR THE POWERLESS

KELLY HALL

We are powerless over what You have not given us power to do—
when we try to manage what we cannot,
we wonder why we lose control.

When I ponder over the things I tighten my grip around the most—
people and things, addictions and dreams—
I sense the long and frayed end of myself.

Help me to accept my eventual death,
my humanity, and the absence of complete control
and turn to You.

Let what does not promote life slough away,
like old skin—
like the shed of fall to winter, and the melt of winter to spring.
Let life and love have its way now,
let life and love spring up along life's path.

STEP ONE

DALE AND JUANITA RYAN

"**We admitted we were powerless over alcohol—that our lives had become unmanageable.** Who cares to admit complete defeat? Practically no one, of course. Every natural instinct cries out against the idea of personal powerlessness. It is truly awful to admit that, glass in hand, we have warped our minds into such an obsession for destructive drinking that only an act of Providence can remove it from us. But upon entering AA, we soon take quite another view of this absolute humiliation. We perceive that only through utter defeat are we able to take our first steps toward liberation and strength. Our admissions of personal powerlessness finally turn out to be firm bedrock upon which happy and purposeful lives may be built."

—*Anonymous,* Twelve Steps and Twelve Traditions

"People in the Twelve-Step programs know that until you're hurting enough, the Steps won't work for you. But for the fortunate sufferer, there comes a time when he or she says, 'I've got to get well. I can't stand living like this anymore.' And that is when one is ready for the miracles of the Twelve Steps."

—*J. Keith Miller,* A Hunger for Healing

In most classrooms, students begin with easy lessons and gradually progress to more difficult ones. In the Twelve Steps, we begin with what some people experience as the most difficult lesson of all: **no matter how powerful we may think we are, we are not powerful enough on our own to do what we want and need to do.** On the surface it may seem like a simple lesson. There is nothing particularly complicated about it.

Experience suggests, however, that it can be a very difficult lesson to learn. Alcoholics Anonymous makes this point simply in Step One: *"We admitted we were powerless over alcohol–that our lives had become unmanageable."*

It is not easy to admit powerlessness. All of us want to maintain the illusion that we can manage our lives on our own. Eventually, however, we must all face the fact that there is a gap between our intentions and our ability to carry them out. This gap shows up in different ways for each of us. We may intend to stop drinking, but find that we are unable to do so for more than short periods of time. We may want to stop turning to food every time we feel sad or anxious, but find ourselves eating far beyond what we intended. We may want to be more expressive of our deepest feelings, but find ourselves emotionally withdrawn. We may promise ourselves that we will spend more time with our children, but continue to allow work to take priority. All of these gaps between our intentions and our actions are evidence of powerlessness.

We attempt to bridge the gap between our intentions and our behavior by trying harder to do things differently. But trying harder doesn't always work. In fact, sometimes the harder we try, the more unmanageable our lives become. Twelve Step programs begin with the admission that we cannot make the changes we need to make by using willpower alone. Whether we believe we are addicted or not, the lie that we are smart enough or competent enough or powerful enough to manage our lives on our own will eventually be shown for what it is—**an attempt to play God**. It takes courage to face our powerlessness. But the admission of powerlessness makes possible a dramatic spiritual change in our lives.

A CLOSER LOOK AT STEP ONE:

We: The first word of Step One implies that healing takes place in community, not in isolation. This is not a new idea: "Two are better than one, because they have a good return for their labor—if either of them falls down, one can help the other up. *But pity anyone who falls and has no one to help them up!"* (Ecclesiastes 4:9-10, NIV, emphasis mine)

The need for community is a major theme in biblical spirituality. God calls us to community, into close relationships with others. All of us are part of God's family, that is why Jesus taught us to pray to "Our Father, who art in heaven . . . ."

Admitted: Spiritual kindergarten begins with the admission that we are in trouble. When we acknowledge this, we are ready to begin our spiritual journey toward peace and serenity. Admitting the truth is not something we can do casually. For most of us, it represents a major change in business-as-usual. We have learned pretense, evasion, and denial. Now we must learn to admit the truth. The Bible puts a high value on telling the truth: "Each of you must put off falsehood and speak truthfully to your neighbor" (Ephesians 4:25). The falsehood that we "put off" in Step One is the belief that we do not need any help, that we can handle it, that we are managing our lives successfully on our own. In Step One we admit that this is not true. To our surprise, when we admit this truth, new and better ways of living become possible for us.

We Were Powerless: Being powerless does not mean that we are incompetent or helpless. Nor does it mean that we have no power at all. It means that we cannot rely on our will alone to achieve wholeness and peace. Willpower alone is not powerful enough. We see our powerlessness when we try to solve a problem through willpower (by determination, commitment, and trying harder), but find that the changes we achieve are only temporary. We may try to control the drinking or drug use of someone we love, but trying, trying harder, and trying our hardest will not make us powerful enough to achieve our objective. Or we may promise to say no to additional responsibilities, only to find ourselves taking on more and more obligations. If you have made promises, decisions, or choices and then found that your determination and commitment were not powerful enough to achieve the desired results, then you know what it is to experience powerlessness. If you have experienced fear or anxiety that you are unable to manage, you know what it is to be powerless. If you hide behind defenses of one kind or another and cannot be at ease with yourself or others, you know what it is to be powerless.

The Apostle Paul talked about powerlessness when he said, "I have the desire to do what is good, but I cannot carry it out" (Romans 7:18). Paul realized that the solution to his problem would need to involve more than just increased willpower. The central point of powerlessness is that willpower alone is not sufficient to enable us to make permanent changes. Trying harder didn't work for the Apostle Paul, and it doesn't work for us either.

Over Alcohol: The word "alcohol" in Step One can be replaced with other substances, behaviors, or conditions. Narcotics Anonymous, for example, replaces "alcohol" with "addictive substances." Some codependency groups replace it with "other people's choices." Some Christians use the word "sin" or "the effects of sin." The use of other words to replace "alcohol" allows anyone to use the Twelve Steps. The basic principles of the Steps are the same no matter what substance or behavior may be the focus of our addictive process.

Our Lives Had Become Unmanageable: What does it mean that our lives are unmanageable? It means that our efforts to manage our lives are not successful. We keep doing the things we think will solve our problems, only to find that our solutions are often worse than our problems ever were. There is an old slogan in AA that summarizes this: "I never had a problem that was worse than the old solution I found for it." Our lives become unmanageable because our "solutions" make things worse. We may eat because we don't want to feel so depressed, but the reality is that compulsive eating makes us more depressed. We may act out sexually because we don't want to feel so lonely, only to find ourselves more alienated than ever. We may run up large debts by buying new clothes so that we will feel less shame, only to feel the added shame that our spending is out of control. Solutions like these do not satisfy us for extended periods of time. The problems always return in one form or another. The prophet Isaiah was on target when he asked, "Why spend money on what is not bread, and your labor on what does not satisfy?" (Isaiah 55:2) Step One invites us to face the fact that our efforts to manage our lives have not worked. We will not be able to find better solutions until we have seen with clarity that our current solutions are part of the problem.

TO BE POWERLESS
JOEL MCKERROW

To be powerless
is to free fall from the cliff top.
The split second of life before the ground.
No choices. No roots. No bounce.
Just you and the air and the knowing of what is to come.
Powerless to change a thing.
Gravity is a force to be reckoned with,
and so is sickness and so is poverty and so is addiction.
They rend us powerless and falling hard
no matter which way is chosen.
Sickness is the first few seconds of falling,
pushed over the cliff by one's own broken body.
There is still hope that a hand may reach out to bring healing.
      Unless it doesn't.
Poverty is the drop that comes after a push.
The rest of the world, it seems, has forced you over
and now reclines above you in the fall.
Yet again there is hope
that someone up there will notice.
Until they don't.
Addiction is a long fall.
You cannot tell if it was others or your own hand that pushed.
Perhaps it was both,
and what does it matter now?
You know there is no one coming
no hand to grab hold,
no one who will notice,
no person who cares.
Until someone does.
Until someone teaches you
that falling
can very easily become flying
with just a few right choices,
just a few precise movements.
Powerlessness can quickly turn its head
and become
surrender.

POOR IN SPIRIT

GREGG TAYLOR

Blessed are the poor in spirit. Isn't that what Jesus says? I've caught myself thinking about this (and some other crazy things Jesus says) and saying to myself, *Really? Does that really work in the world we live in? Does that really work in this thing I call my life?*

But can you imagine a world where no one is poor in spirit? I wonder what would that be like. Our total experience of life—our relationships with each other and with God, the way we spend our money, relate to people, parent, date, church, pray, marry, work, handle conflict, and try to put the broken pieces of our lives back together—would be totally consumed and controlled by arrogance, self-promotion, dishonesty, self-deception, and conflict.

Can you imagine a world where no one is poor in spirit? There would be
 . . . no humility from anyone.
 . . . no caring for one another.
 . . . no real community.
 . . . no experience of belonging.
 . . . no forgiving each other.
 . . . no reconciliation of broken relationships between husbands and wives, dads and sons, mothers and daughters, or friends who have gotten crossways or sideways or without a way with each other.

Can you imagine a world where no one is poor in spirit? There would be
 . . . no authentic communication between people.
 . . . no giving, no generosity of spirit.
 . . . no clothing the naked, feeding the hungry, visiting the prisoner, welcoming the stranger.

Can you imagine a world where no one is poor in spirit? There would be
  . . . no recovery from addiction.
  . . . no peace in our world.
  . . . no peace in our hearts.
  . . . no healing of relationships.
  . . . no light in the dark recesses of our souls.
  . . . no celebrating someone else's success.
  . . . no gratitude.
  . . . no compassion for someone else's pain.

Can you imagine a world where no one is poor in spirit? There would be
  . . . no one saying, "I'm sorry."
  . . . no one saying, "I forgive you."
  . . . no one saying, "Will you forgive me?"
  . . . no one saying, "Thank you."
  . . . no one taking responsibility for the harm they've caused
       someone else.
  . . . no one making amends for the wreckage they've wrecked.
  . . . no one holding a door open for someone else.
  . . . no one waiting for you.
  . . . no one praying for you.
  . . . no one welcoming the prodigal home.

Can you imagine a world where no one is poor in spirit? There would be
  . . . no Jesus and no cross and no resurrection.
  . . . no access to God—we would be our own gods.
  . . . no faith, hope, or love. These three would not remain.
  . . . a perpetual state of war with others.

Can you imagine a world where no one is poor in spirit? There would
be no . . .
  Oh . . . wait.
  Maybe that's the point.

"I know that in me, that is, in my fallen human nature, there is nothing good. I can will myself to do something good, but that does not help me carry it out. I can determine that I am going to do good, but I don't do it; instead, I end up living out the evil that I decided not to do. If I end up doing the exact thing I pledged not to do, I am no longer doing it because sin has taken up residence in me.

"Here's an *important* principle I've discovered: regardless of my desire to do the right thing, *it is clear that* evil is never far away. For deep down I am in happy agreement with God's law; but the rest of me does not concur. I see a very different principle at work in my bodily members, and it is at war with my mind; I have become a prisoner in this war to the rule of sin in my body."

—*Romans 7:18-23*, The Voice

DOOMED

JAMES RYAN

Currently, the highlight of my spiritual practice is the Big Book study that I run on Wednesday mornings at a local recovery house. Two weeks back, we were reading a bit of the book *More About Alcoholism*. Just after Jim, just before Fred.

The insane idea won out.

The book was introducing "mental obsession," and the residents didn't seem at all impressed. Nobody volunteered anything. No one, apparently, identified.

So I put it like this: "The book starts out by telling us that we can't drink safely; we have an allergy. Now it's telling us that our minds are broken and will make us drink even if we don't want to. So what do we do about that?"

I didn't expect anyone to answer that question. But they did.

Everyone did.

They all had something to share, some idea about how the mental obsession could be handled:

"Meetings, meetings, meetings. That's what I need."

"You just have to pick up that ten thousand pound phone."

"Next time, I'll just have to play the tape through to the end."

"No one ever drank who got on their knees and prayed in the morning."

"I know that if I stick with the winners, I'll be okay."

"I think I'll take a coffee commitment."

"Think, think, think . . . "

On and on they went, these residents, none with more than thirty days on the wagon, but each with a firmly entrenched idea of what staying sober was all about. Many of them were cycling through the house for the second or third time, still selling the same garbage they collected on their last run through.

Not an unusual experience. Many groups go this way. The program isn't an easy thing to catch hold of. It's simple, but hard on the ego. So it's no surprise that a roomful of drunks and drug addicts would have a skewed view of the program.

What struck me that morning, though, was the fact that each solution they came up with was something accepted by most AAs as good program. Everything I heard that morning from the mouths of the newly sober was something I'd heard many times from clubhouse old timers, the guys with their own mugs hanging from hooks on the wall. But it wasn't keeping these guys sober. And it wasn't program.

If you can't drink and you can't *not* drink, and somebody asks you what you're going to do about it, there is only one right answer: *Nothing.*

Bill used to talk about a thing called "deflation at depth," and this is exactly what he meant by that: there isn't a damned thing you can do to keep yourself sober.

It's a terrible blow to the ego.

But if we can take that blow fully, if we can let it knock our egos to the mat, even for a short count, it opens up the very real possibility of contact with supernatural power.

Short of total defeat, there is no possibility of contact. If we aren't defeated, then we're still trying to make a go of it on our own.

Anything, absolutely anything, we do to keep ourselves sober immediately closes that window of opportunity. Even going to meetings. Even working the Steps. Even helping other alcoholics. Even prayer.

The ego is a subtle foe, and it will use anything it can get its hands on, even the best parts of our program, to haul itself back up into the saddle.

The only appropriate response to temptation is to stop everything and just take a minute to be doomed.

Let it sink in. Let it wash over you. And for God's sake, don't fight it.

I haven't had a drink or a drug in seven years. In 2001 my sponsor took me through the Big Book, and I had a powerful, transformative experience. This experience did not make me immune to lapses in judgment, fits of unwillingness, or even occasional temptation.

At two years sober, I saw a guy smoke pot in a movie and it gave me the shivers. At five years, I was in a bad way and caught myself planning a trip to the bar. Then at seven years, just a few days before this particular Wednesday morning, I was transfixed by a realization of just how much I enjoyed getting high.

That's three times in seven years that I should have fallen off the wagon and didn't.

At two years, my response was to run into the next room, get on my knees and pray. Then I wrote a bunch of inventory, read it, and made an amend. At five years, my response was to force myself to go to meetings I hadn't been to before. Then I wrote a bunch of inventory, read it, and made an amend.

Each response was the very best program I could come up with; each response was a panicked one, an act of desperation. And I remained shaken for weeks afterward, questioning my program and my connection with God. What was wrong with me? Where was I screwing up the program? What could I do to get it right?

Maybe it's easier to be doomed on day one than on day 1,958. Maybe getting some time under my belt made me think I ought to know better and should have had this thing handled by now. After all, I had all the tools, right? I just had to use them to put myself back together again.

Only that's not how the tools work.

These tools don't work if you're the one using them.

At seven years, my response was to stop everything. Sit quietly. Be doomed.

No "think, think, thinking" about anything at all. No panicked race for a notebook or a church basement. No phone calls.

Just doom.

I cannot fix this.

It's a terrible feeling. But it joined me, hard and fast, to the presence of God.

WHAT I LEARNED WHILE OUR SON WAS STILL USING DRUGS

JUANITA RYAN

Children are some of our best teachers. They teach us, experientially, to open our hearts, give of ourselves, seek wisdom, set limits, embrace, and let go. Children never stop teaching us. But as with most of life, the greatest lessons often seem to come during the toughest times.

The year our oldest son dropped out of high school and became an addict was a very dark and difficult year for us. It was also a time of deeper exposure to life's most important lessons. I didn't fully realize it until much later, but it was during that anguished time that our son taught me a greater understanding of humility, honesty, courage, trust, and grace.

HUMILITY

Humility is, in many ways, the opposite of shame. Shame causes us to judge and attack ourselves for our limits and weaknesses, leaving us scrambling to hide or pretend or try harder. Humility, on the other hand, does not make negative judgments about our limits and weaknesses, but instead embraces them as reality—as simply what is. Shame pushes us to say, *I should*, even in the face of our powerlessness. Humility frees us to say, *I cannot*, when we are faced with things that are beyond our control.

When our son was using, I thought I should be able to do all kinds of things that I could not do. Intellectually I knew better. Even experientially I knew better. But this was my child. Everything in me seemed to insist I should.

I should be able to figure out when he was using and when he was not. *I should* be able to reason with him. *I should* be able to make him stop. *I should* be able to keep him away from his using friends. *I should* be able to get him the right help. *I should* be able to protect him from harm, including his self-harm.

I tried. For months, I tried. But I could not do any of these things. Believing I should be able to do what I could not do, and endlessly trying to control what I could not control, left me in my own insanity. It was only when I grew sick and tired of my own insanity that I was able to recognize that my life had become unmanageable. And it was only then that I was ready to learn new lessons in humility.

Humility helped to restore my sanity. I could not do for my son any of what I, as his parent, wanted so desperately to do. I could not. That simple truth was excruciatingly painful and yet wonderfully freeing. Recognizing this is what ultimately opened the door for my healing and for the healing of our family, because healing could occur only when I lived in that humble truth and got out of God's way. I stopped trying to do what only God could do when I humbly admitted, *I cannot.*

"Blessed are the poor in spirit," Jesus taught us, "for theirs is the kingdom of heaven" (Matthew 5:3, NIV). We open ourselves to receiving God's healing in our lives when we come to the end of trying to control what we cannot control. Every time we acknowledge our spiritual poverty (our creaturely dependence on our loving Maker) and live in the truth of our need for God, the kingdom of heaven is ours. When we let ourselves be who we are as God's much loved children, and let God be God, the doors and windows of our lives are thrown open for us to receive God and all of God's love, life, and goodness into our lives. This is the amazing grace of true humility. It is the central dynamic of the first three steps of the Twelve Steps.

HONESTY

Honesty is the capacity to tell the truth about ourselves. It is the ability and choice to let ourselves and others know what we are observing, what we can and can't do, what we are thinking and feeling, what we are wanting, and what our behaviors have been. Honesty is reality unadorned, the truth with no spin. What Jesus taught us about the truth is that it will set us free.

Honesty is the twin sister of humility. It is the freedom to let go of attempts to manage what others think of us. It is the relief that comes with being real about our limits, flaws, poor choices, sin, fears, shame, longings, and love. It is the joy of being able to let go of our self-image, allowing ourselves to be ordinary human beings.

The truth we need to let ourselves know and speak is, most importantly, the truth about ourselves. The first step of honesty that I had the opportunity to take when our son was using drugs, was to stop focusing on his insanity about drugs and to focus instead on my insanity about him. In my attempts to control what was beyond my control, I was playing God. As a result, I became increasingly out of touch with reality, obsessed, and irrational. I had to admit my own insanity before any positive change could take place.

The second step of honesty became possible for me once I admitted that I could not control what was out of my control. Paradoxically, this admission allowed me to take a much clearer look at the significance of what was happening. There was a problem. Our son was in trouble. I had to stop minimizing and denying this truth. I had to see and admit to myself, to God, and to others the existence of this problem. And I had to let myself see clearly its enormity, its progressive nature, and its life-threatening reality.

The third step of honesty I needed to take was to acknowledge that I was a part of the problem. This can be tricky territory because we often want to take either no responsibility or total responsibility for other people's behavior. And because usually neither of these is the truth, we end up in confusion and continued chaos. I had to sort out what was and what was *not* my part of the problem.

The clarity that humility brought me made it easier for me to see that the choices my son was making were not my doing. I was not forcing the drugs into him. He was doing this; I was not. I did not cause these choices; I could not control these choices. His addiction was his problem.

There were ways, however, in which I was a part of the problem. First,

I was part of the problem because I had passed on burdens of shame, fear, and guilt to my son long before I knew that I carried these burdens myself. Like all parents, there were ways I had hurt my son and had failed him. The inherited burdens of shame, fear, guilt, and unresolved pain that he carried were, in part, what made him more vulnerable to self-destructive choices.

Second, I was part of the problem because I continued to try to fix or control my son and his problem. In doing this, I continued to slip back into minimizing or denying his drug use, wanting to avoid the truth because I didn't want to face the pain.

Third, I was part of the problem because I was not taking good care of myself. I was so busy with all the insanity of the situation that I neglected some of my own basic needs.

Telling myself, God, and a few other people these basic truths helped to free me from adding more shame, fear, and guilt to my life, and our son's. Honesty freed me from getting lost in self-blame or from needlessly blaming others. Shame and blame only add to the problem. Telling the truth, however, is like shining a light in the dark; it brings simplicity and clarity. What became simply and clearly evident when I told the truth was that there was a problem of great significance—our son needed help, I needed help, our family needed help. Truth, when we find it, is always freeing.

COURAGE

Courage is the capacity to take action in spite of fear. Courage does not feel like freedom from fear, because it is not. The fear is still there. Courage is choosing not to allow fear to decide for us what we will and will not do. Courage is the God-given strength to make decisions based on the wisdom we have gained from humility and honesty, rather than from fear.

The serenity prayer teaches us to pray for the serenity to accept what we cannot change, the courage to change what we can, and the wisdom to know the difference. Accepting the truth about my son's problem, and about my inability to change or control him, led me to see the things I *could* change. I could not change him, but perhaps I could, with God's help, change myself. I was a part of the problem. Perhaps I could be a part of the solution as well.

One thing I could change was taking better care of myself. It took some courage to begin caring for myself because in this situation I sometimes confused self-care with selfishness and was tempted to berate myself for even the most basic acts of self-care. But self-care is always a gift to ourselves and to other people in our lives because it fosters self-respect and respect of others, and it allows us to live more sanely.

At the time, taking better care of myself meant not living my life obsessed about our son's choices, but allowing myself to pursue my own life. It meant spending time alone with God and time alone with my husband. It meant spending time with our other son and spending time with friends. Taking care of myself also meant getting all the help and support I needed so that I could continue living in humility and honesty. All of this took courage because I was afraid that if I moved my primary focus off our son and onto my life, I was in some way abandoning him, and that might make his problems worse.

When I took better care of myself, I began to notice my limits. Our son was living in our home and he was often up all night. His behavior was erratic. He had days of paranoia and times when he lashed out at us verbally. All of this was not only painful to watch but very disruptive to our lives. Because of my ongoing self-care, I began to see clearly that I could not go on living that way.

The day came when my husband and I agreed that we could not continue to live that way any more. We contacted a treatment center to secure a place in their program and then sat down with our beloved son, who was terribly paranoid by this time. We told him that we loved him but could not continue to live with his drug use. We told him that he needed to either go to this treatment program or move out on his own. We knew that moving out on his own would mean he would be on the streets, loaded and paranoid. Our fear was so great that we felt like our hearts would stop. And yet, by God's grace, we found the courage to do the sanest thing we had done in months. God granted us the courage we needed to change what we could change, to tell the truth, and to speak from humility rather than from shame or blame.

If we had allowed our fears to be the guiding principle of our decision-making, the chaos and insanity of our lives and of our son's life would most likely have continued. But when we humbly told the truth about our limits, when we accepted that we could not stop or control our son's drug use, and when we were granted the courage to change what we could by asking him to go into treatment or move out, new possibilities for healing were opened for all of us. This particular act of courage required that I learn another vital life lesson, the lesson of trust.

TRUST

Trust is the ability to rely or depend on another person's help, support, and care. In the second of the Twelve Steps, we come to believe that a Power greater than ourselves can restore us to sanity. In the third step, we make the decision to turn our lives and wills over to the loving, capable care of God. We make the decision to trust God.

I have heard this short catch phrase—"Trust God"—all my life. It is said all too often as a kind of magical spell, a quick fix. It seems to be thrown out as an easy answer by people who haven't even bothered to listen to the problem. *Trust God. What did it mean? How does one do this? What does it change?* More often than not, it seemed to lead to shame and confusion rather than to restored lives.

When our son was addicted to drugs, lying about his use, and growing more and more paranoid, "Trust God" took on an entirely new and desperate meaning for me. What I was hearing through the phrase was, "Let go of your son even though it feels like he will fall to his death. Let go of him and trust that God will catch and hold and care for him." I felt like I was being asked to do the impossible.

But it is what I had to do. I could no longer put my trust in my abilities to fix the problem. Only God could restore our son. My work was to entrust our son, myself, and our entire family to God's loving care. Every day. Multiple times a day. Trusting God was no longer a simple slogan. It took on urgent meaning. It became something visceral. At first it was like performing a high-wire act, expecting to fall at any moment, but choosing to believe that there was a safety net beneath us even though I could not see the net or understand how it could catch us.

So what steps did I take as I inched my way out onto that high wire? I prayed. Not long, theologically correct prayers, but short, urgent prayers for help, guidance, and courage. I asked others who knew and loved us to pray for us as well. I accepted the seriousness of the problem we faced as a family, as well as our powerlessness to cure addiction. Ultimately, we required that our son go into treatment or move out. That was the moment when we actively, fully let him go and entrusted him to God's care.

In the midst of our darkest days, a friend who was praying for us told me that she sensed God was inviting me to rest. Rest! The word startled me. It seemed so bizarre in my circumstances. And yet I could feel the difference it would make. I could climb down from my imaginary high-wire act and crawl into God's loving arms. And rest. For me this became the deepest, truest meaning of the word trust. And it, too, was visceral—this sense of being securely held in the arms of love, that everyone in my family was being held by God. I did not have to let my son fall; he was held. Letting him go simply meant that I stopped getting in God's way, that I quit acting as if there were no God waiting to heal my son. Letting go meant resting in God's powerful love for me and for my son.

It was a gift of grace that our son agreed, reluctantly, to go into treatment. This might not have been the outcome of our intervention. He might have decided to spend time on the streets before he became willing to end the nightmare. There is no way to know in advance how long the journey with addiction will go on. It is not something we can control. But, fortunately, that was not his choice. We found out later that he decided to go to treatment partly because he had become so paranoid that he wanted to get away from the people he thought were after him. God used the insanity he was experiencing to help him make a sane choice.

The outcome of the story is that by letting our son go, we got him back. God brought healing to our son and our family one day at a time, day after day after day. "It is a story of redemption," our son said a few years later. I agree—a story of redemption, a story full of grace.

GRACE

Grace is the healing, saving, blessing activity of God in our lives. Grace is God being God. It is God with us.

I learned grace in new ways while our son was still using. I experienced God with us in that dark time. God did not wait until we had everything figured out—not at all. God was with us through it all, in it all, extending healing and blessing. It was God's grace that drew us into humility and honesty, God's grace that gave us courage when our hearts grew faint with fear, and God's grace that taught us to entrust ourselves and our son to God's loving care.

Sometimes people define grace as "unmerited favor" and then go on to talk about grace as if it were something God extends to us in spite of our lack of value in God's eyes. I experienced deeply that this is not what grace is at all. Unmerited favor (or unearned favor) means that grace is something we cannot earn because it is already ours. God's grace and love are ours. Already. Always. Unmerited favor means that God's loving-kindness toward us does not change as we change. It is constant and unchangeable, and therefore, absolutely reliable. Grace is God always seeing and knowing our infinite value. Grace is God actively seeking to awaken us to God's love for us and to our everlasting value to God.

When our son was at his worst, his value, his preciousness in our eyes never changed. We loved and treasured him. If we, being broken parents, could extend that kind of grace to our son without even trying, how much more does God's love of us never fail? This is the grace I experienced in new ways while our son was still using.

Jesus told a story in which God is a parent whose child has lost his way. This is a familiar story: the son has taken his portion of the inheritance and quickly spent it all, most likely on mood-altering behaviors. The father looks down the road day after day, filled with longing for this son he loves and values beyond measure. The father endlessly scans the horizon for his son, waiting for the day his son will return. The father never forgets his son's infinite value or his own endless love for him. So when the son first appears far off down the road, the father runs toward him with arms outstretched and joy in his heart. The father does not listen to the son's rehearsed speech about not being worthy; instead, the father demonstrates to the son the son's great value. The father throws his arms around his son, embracing him in love and gladness. Then the father places his ring on his son's finger, his coat on his son's shoulders, and tells his servants to prepare a party in honor of his son. This is grace. It is God's extravagant, unshakable valuing and loving of us. This is God's grace toward us as parents. This is God's grace toward our children. This is God's never-ending grace toward each and every one of us.

Humility. Honesty. Courage. Trust. Grace. These lessons were both hard won and pure gift. I am grateful beyond telling for our son's recovery and for our recovery as a family. And I am deeply and every-day grateful for the life lessons God taught me while our son was still using drugs.

May the God of grace keep you all in peace. May you, by God's grace, know the freedom of humility and honesty, and the possibilities of courage and trust. May God's grace bring full healing to you and to those you love.

POWERLESS AS A PARENT

ANDY GULLAHORN

Our first child was a pretty easy baby. He slept through the night after a couple of months. He smiled all the time. He didn't cry very much. We were pretty sure that we had figured out the perfect parenting style. All of those other parents who had difficult babies must not have been gifted with our expert parental instincts.

Then we had two more kids.

There is nothing like having multiple children to show you how powerless you really are. Sure, we still try to steer our kids' lives in numerous ways, but ultimately there are so many things that are and will always be out of our control. It was one thing to find myself powerless over the life of my child and another thing to eventually recognize the powerlessness I have over my own self. But much in the same way, there can be great freedom when I accept my limitations and trust that power is in the hands of a God whose loving parental instincts stretch beyond my comprehension.

DESPERATE MAN

A SONG

ANDY GULLAHORN

I know I just display my foolish pride
When I try to be an island to myself
You must be tired of all the stuff that I still hide
Cause I just can't seem to trust anyone else

It's a lonely way to live
Such a lonely way to live

I'm a desperate man
I'm in desperate need
Of Your saving hand to come and rescue me

You've been more than patient all this time
If it were me, I would've given up long ago
The first time that You pulled me from the mire
And I brushed you off to dig another hole

It's a sad way to live
Such a sad, sad way to live

I'm a desperate man
I'm in desperate need
Of Your saving hand to come and rescue me

I used to be the strong one
The self-sufficient fool
I thought I needed no one
But the plain and simple truth
Is I'm a desperate man

I'm a desperate man
I'm in desperate need
Of Your saving hand to come and rescue me

DOWNLOAD LINK:
HTTPS://DL.DROPBOXUSERCONTENT.COM/U/13922983/DESPERATEMAN.MP3

"God's strength shows up in my weakness as soon as I recognize my weakness."

—Aaron Edwards

"Come close to the one true God, and He will draw close to you. Wash your hands; you have dirtied them in sin. Cleanse your heart, because your mind is split down the middle, *your love for God on one side and selfish pursuits on the other.*"

—James 4:8, The Voice

EMPTYING

KATHY MCDOUGALL-YEAGER

I lay down my rights
the right to happiness
the right to be right
the right to make you make me feel happy
the right to make you be or do anything
I lay down my right to fix
I lay down my right to make
to try
to create what can only be created through HIM
to create what can only be corrupted by my efforts
I lay down my attempts
I lay down my control
I lay down my will in the matter
my opinion
my goals
my hope
I lay down everything
And commit only to exist
Untidy
Unkempt
Unfulfilled
Longing
Chaotic
Echoing an ancient cry
Of hollow discontent
Empty
In a posture of waiting
To be filled.

REARRANGING ROOMS

TERESA McBEAN

I am suffering, and if you were my friend, you'd agree that this is about right, considering my circumstances. Last week a beloved member of our faith family over-dosed and died. He wasn't as famous as Phillip Seymour Hoffman, but he was precious to us, and we are sad. (We feel strangely connected and aggrieved over the loss of Hoffman, too.) One of our favorite seventeen-year-olds in our community was diagnosed with two nasty forms of sarcoma (usually reserved only for the old and infirm) and is undergoing brutal treatment. My mom's dementia is slowly taking her away, although her physical presence often tricks me into hoping otherwise.

These are recent examples of real life teaching me that I am power-less and have no control in any dimension of my life. I'm even powerless over the way I cope with my struggles—and annoyingly unaware of this most of the time. You see, I'm the kind of gal who not only repurposes furniture, but repurposes rooms. No one knows which room will be the dining room or the den on any given day. It took a while to figure out that moving the furniture was about more than aesthetics. I used to make up a lot of excuses about why I was so committed to chaos, but today I acknowledge that I rearrange rooms in response to my suffer-ing. It's a way for me to experience some control, I suppose, especially when I feel a complete loss of it in important areas of my life and min-istry. Like when someone commits suicide or relapses, or my kid comes home with a tattoo.

Last Saturday morning, my husband scanned the sports listings and determined which events he was going to watch on his day off. A couple of his favorite teams were playing, and he was eager to watch every minute of each event. I interrupted his fantasies by saying, "I want to rearrange two, maybe four rooms today. I want to put the dining room back to where it was in 1999, and I want to move the armoire from the guest bedroom into our master. I am sick of the piano in the playroom, can we move it to the den?"

This is no rookie husband. We've been married thirty-five years. He didn't respond with, "I would like to call your attention to the fact that you have had a hard, long week of suffering. I know you are stressed out, grieving for the loss of our friend. You are probably worried what the autopsy is going to reveal. You are really stressed out about people we love who are sick and suffering. Instead of moving furniture, why don't we pray?" My guy didn't say any of these true things.

"Which room do you want to start with?" He said, with barely a sigh.

We pushed and pulled, dragged and adjusted area rugs and sofas, lamps and end tables. I placed a comfy chair right next to the fireplace. My beloved said not a word about having to move a jillion pound dining room table into another room to accomplish this feat. Because my husband granted me grace (he knows that he is powerless over my compulsions) and helped me shove rooms into new configurations, I was soon freed to sit next to a cozy fire. As I grew still, I became conscious of my own powerlessness over my compulsions. This awareness was not forced upon me, but came over me as I sat in silent prayer. "Oh my, I rearranged the furniture because I feel so anxious and worried, sorrowful and sad."

Powerlessness works like this: it doesn't try to control or demand its own way. Pete, my husband, was practicing a lifestyle choice of powerlessness. He didn't try to fix me, demand that I change, or even ask me to tell him how I was really feeling. He served me, and in so doing, sat with me in my pain.

Too bad I didn't return the favor. After all that manual labor, we decided to hit the gym for a quick cardio workout before heading out to our evening worship service. We weren't even out of the driveway before he began making suggestions about how I might improve my care and handling of our CDs. He talked to me about the value of returning a CD to its proper case. He had opened one expecting Bruce Springsteen, and was surprised and disappointed to find, instead, the Muppet Christmas compilation (for some crazy reason, this seemed to bother him. Husbands. What can you do?)

A good wife, one married for over three decades, might have paused to prepare. Maybe a decent partner, having had her own experience with grief just a few short hours prior, would have had the discernment to realize that her man was suffering also. Maybe his sense of powerlessness was popping out in a vain attempt to exert control over my careless treatment of any CD I ever touch.

But I am not a good wife. I took his comments personally, and returned his "suggestions" with some well-worn and often recycled spousal ammunition of my own. "Well goodness, if I had known you cared so much about a clean car, I would expect you to wash this one once or twice a year, whether it needs it or not." We made it to the gym and went our separate, cranky ways.

There are a million ways we try to distract ourselves from suffering. Most of us grieving types would give our favorite coffee mug to anyone who could tell us how to access just one of those million ways to get the pain to stop.

In a grief support group that I attend, our facilitator suggested that suffering delayed makes the heart sick. In an attempt to get us grievers to sit with our pain, we were given a list of words: agony, blue devils, blues, dejection, depression, desolateness, desolation, despair, disconsolateness, distress, doldrums, dumps, joylessness, melancholy, misery, pain, self-reproach, self-pity, shame, suffering, torment, and wretchedness, to name a few. Then she asked us to sit with these words and try to circle the ones that applied to our own experience. Three people got up and left the meeting. According to grief gurus, we stumble over our healing when we try to either ignore or solve our suffering. Imagine three people walking out of a grief group they voluntarily attend when they were asked to . . . feel.

Pete and I can imagine walking out, but we have chosen instead the lifestyle of powerlessness. After working up a good sweat, we were able to return to the scene of the crime—our car—and express more truthfully our mutual sorrow over our attempts to control each other. It wasn't pretty, but we managed to get through our own limitations and return to a place of mutual care and concern.

This is our work as a couple, as well as within our faith community. We do not show up and tell one another why we are the way we are, but do the work necessary to be fully present for each other *when* we are the way we are. And on the days we can stand it, we are going to nudge one another to accept a different (and I pray) more inspired way of seeing.

Maybe that's the ultimate point of powerlessness. It's not an explanation for why we seek control rather than surrender. It's not an excuse for rude and bad behavior. It's an exercise and really quite a grand privilege. Powerlessness is an opportunity to be more honest with ourselves, God, and others about the truth of who we are—and I find that quite a hopeful place to reside, even as I suffer.

"God pays attention when people come to the end of their resources. God draws near in those times."

—*Dale Ryan*

"For what the Law was powerless to do because it was weakened by the flesh, God did by sending his own Son in the likeness of sinful flesh to be a sin offering. And so he condemned sin in the flesh."

— *Romans 8:3,* NIV

POWERLESSNESS
AS A PRACTICE

SCOTT McBEAN

Powerlessness is one of the most fundamental concepts of recovery (and spirituality for that matter), and yet for me it remains elusive because I don't know how to be powerless.

By and large, I can manage quite of few of the problems I currently face. My life has been, at times, far more unmanageable than it is in its current state. There are a variety of reasons for that. One of those reasons is that, somehow, in the midst of total unmanageability, I was able to find a way to begin the process of surrendering my life to God's care and control. I've been taught the importance of surrendering daily. I've been told many times never to forget the importance of utter reliance on God for protection, guidance, safety, security, and whatever else I need to get me from one day to the next. And when life crumbles and we face these times of complete exhaustion and unmanageability, I find that daily surrender is much more achievable simply because I have no other choice.

That's why, today, I have a dilemma. I do not feel as powerless over my life circumstances. Perhaps, in a way, that makes me lucky. I do feel rather lucky in this moment. It's certainly a good thing to be able to say that life has moved from a state of complete unmanageability to one of serenity. I'm trying to embrace that now because I recognize it probably will not last forever. Times of greater powerlessness and unmanageability are inevitably bound to come.

Though I'm frightened as I write these thoughts, because I know what they might mean. Perhaps I'm setting myself up for trouble. I'm lulling myself into a state of complacency. I'm in a phase of life where

I do not have to practice reliance on God because things are, by and large, in place. (Well, they're as "in place" as life circumstances can get.)

I do not mean to say that we don't need to be reliant when things are going well—of course we do—I only mean to say that I do not have to practice being reliant because my circumstances aren't forcing me into that place of daily surrender, as they often have in the past. I recognize this is merely a phase, but that does not mean my recognition will help me avoid the pitfalls of "powerful" living. Somewhere, deep down, I realize the challenge of embracing powerlessness is maintaining the discipline to recognize how powerless I am even when my life is not in its most unmanageable place.

I suspect what I'm describing is the difficult tension we sense in recovery: we must struggle to take responsibility for our lives even as we admit to the fact that we aren't really in control. It seems like a paradox, doesn't it? For instance, it is important for me to find ways to daily surrender myself to God's care and control. It is my responsibility to posture myself towards God and live in a powerless kind of way, regardless of my circumstances. Otherwise, as I said, I run the risk of losing sight of who is really in charge.

But if my goal is powerlessness, wouldn't this mean that taking responsibility is just another example of my own efforts to control my world and my life? It's possible! I can't really be sure. I don't know myself well enough to always determine my exact intent or motivation. Am I taking responsibility because I truly desire to work a thorough and earnest recovery program? Or am I taking responsibility so that I can keep feeding my subconscious control issues while I look like I'm working a thorough recovery program? I wish I knew.

I want to work an honest and thorough recovery program. I want to live in a place of daily surrender. At times, I will need to take responsibility over these things. I don't know how to strike that balance best and I don't always know when I'm slipping up. I'm not always aware of my tendencies to slide into complacency. I'm not always honest, yet I don't always know that sometimes I'm dishonest. These are some of the issues I have regardless of my life circumstances. They require me to live humbly and to recognize my own powerlessness before God and over my life. I pray that, no matter what else is going on in my life, I can always recognize how powerless I am over my own attempts to live powerlessly. With all this confusion, mixed with small doses of clarity, I begin to awake to the possibility that powerlessness is not an excuse to live irresponsibly, or an explanation for why I often do what I do not want to do. It's a lifestyle.

AN IRISH VERSION OF THE SERENITY PRAYER

God, take and receive my liberty,
my memory, my understanding and will,
All that I am and have He has given me

God, grant me the serenity
to accept the things I cannot change,
Courage to change the things I can,
And wisdom to know the difference

Living one day at a time
Enjoying one moment at a time
Accepting hardships as the pathway to peace
Taking, as He did, this sinful world as it is,
Not as I would have it

Trusting that He will make all things right
If I surrender to His will
That I may be reasonably happy in this life
and supremely happy in the next.

PEOPLE PLEASING

KELLY HALL

As a teen, I took on a caregiver archetype in my family. I was the "fixer." Somehow, over time, this morphed into a habitual practice of helping or pleasing others so that I could feel safe and accepted. As far as people-pleasing addictions go, I had it good—or bad, whichever you prefer, I want you to feel comfortable *wink*. If asked or complimented about it, I would simply say, "You are totally worth it!"—if I said anything at all. I would never have imagined that people pleasing (my absolute co-dependent behavior) could be so hazardous to my health, until my addiction began to ruin me.

About a decade ago, I was friends with a very sweet woman. She had two children around the same ages as mine, and we would meet up and let them play while we chatted about life. She was a good person, kind and thoughtful, a bit skittish at times though. She also had a lot of secrets—a lifetime of abuse from her alcoholic father, and during that time, at the hands of her addict husband. One night, she lost control, killed her husband and dragged his body into a hole that he himself had dug in the back yard. She buried him with bags of dirt. There was a week-long cover up before she finally confessed to her family and was taken to a hospital, and then directly to jail. One of the last things she did before going to the hospital was call me and, without ever letting me know what happened, say, "We'll always be friends, right?" Of course I agreed we would because I loved her, and besides, after such a bizarre series of both faked and real events that happened that week, I was concerned for her as well. "Remember that," is all she said back to me before hanging up.

When she was released on bond, she came over. I was terrified. She made jokes about the situation, trying to ease the tension, but the room just wouldn't diffuse. "My mom said I have lost a lot of weight . . . Yeah, about 180 pounds!" Crickets. She visited often, and at first I was okay with it. Even though I was scared, I wanted to be supportive. She was not allowed to tell me the whole story, so I was getting bits and pieces from the news and putting it all together. My extended family was a wreck about it all. They would argue her innocence or guilt, and it was all sensational. Many people who loved me wanted me to cease contact with her—"the murderer"—but I didn't know how to draw healthy boundaries. I mean, she was a poor, lost, abused wreck of a soul that needed me, and besides, what if she hated me for abandoning her? I did say we'd always be friends, remember?

While awaiting her trial, she was at my house almost daily, and I began to lose touch with reality. My anxiety was running high. This was my first relationship with a murderer, and I was sore afraid, and yet I couldn't manage to say what I needed to say in order to take care of myself and my family. I would even berate myself: "Look, this girl has gotten a bad rep. She was abused as a child and as a wife, and she just snapped. She killed him in a fit of insanity and couldn't stop herself. She lost control."

As the details of the murder came to light through media, it was more obvious that there was time and room for reality in her insanity. It wasn't a one-blow-kill-its-over kind of thing; it wasn't a passionate struggle. She tied him to a bed and stabbed him two hundred times. It was hard to absorb. It took days and longer to really absorb the truth. Even after learning all this, I couldn't turn her away. I couldn't say no to anyone, not even someone with a proven violent streak.

Sometime during her wait for trial, my youngest sister-in-law was being confirmed. My friend insisted that she babysit for me while we went to the church for the service. My murderous friend who stabbed her husband two hundred times wanted to babysit my children. Onset hives.

"Okay."

I remember sitting in the church without any blood whatsoever. I couldn't believe that my children were at home with a murderer out on bond. What was happening to me? My other sister-in-law left immediately and went to be at my house with her and the kids. Thank God for her sanity, because I had clearly lost mine. To this day I have nightmares.

This is all so hard to admit.

I began to shut down because I couldn't see a way out of my situation. I was powerless over my addiction to please people, to be a good friend like I said I would. I remember locking all the doors and windows, and checking them repeatedly. I remember the sudden panic attacks in the middle of days, meals, nights, or times when the kids were just in another room and I rushed to check on them. She would show up at random times; it was so unpredictable. I tried to be away from home as much as possible unless my husband was home with me.

She began to feel the difference in our relationship. I was tense to say the least. She tried to ask questions and have life be "normal," but there was no way. I went on medication. It was a hard, hard time. I had no other tools in my toolbox to pull from besides avoidance, so I simply avoided her until she got the hint. Awful.

I couldn't fix any of this. This was my first awareness of my powerlessness. Maybe I had encountered it before, but I must have denied it and just rerouted life through control. I was beginning to learn that I couldn't change my past choices, or the happenstances that created the underlying issues that drove me to please people until my life became unmanageable. I certainly couldn't fix her situation. I can't manage what people think of me. I came to the end of myself, the very end. I was out of control. I started therapy.

Over time I came to discover the deep-down wounds that drove my behavior. The self-doubt, the inability to make a decision without worrying what "they" would think. Though really, what I was worried about was what I would think of myself. The drive to put everything in my life on hold for others. I could see how my young life had trained me to be where I was at, how I felt threatened by uncertainty, trying to control everyone's happiness (or at least their happiness with me) so that I could feel safe. I was living a life of regret management, something that I now, ironically, regret.

I also saw how being the "good friend" was cemented into my ego/identity. I liked being her until I was exhausted, felt used, felt like I fell short, or until I just didn't like being that paranoid person anymore.

I joined a church, which seemed the right thing to do.

Going to church didn't cure my addiction, though. In fact it confused the situation quite a bit because of the whole "give your life away to service" idea. So at my new church with my new friends I just kept right on doing my work of pleasing and fitting in, of needing people to need me, only now I was even more justified in it because it made me a "good" Christian. I was convinced to try extreme fad diets and was hospitalized. I tried to give up all man-made materials, even my television. I drove hundreds of miles to put my kids in one school, or pulled them out and moved them to another, or homeschooled. You name it, I gave it a shot. No one even asked me for any of it! I gave up my free time, my family time, and my marriage time all because people "needed me" and I "needed them." I always allowed others to feel right in a disagreement, even if I believed I was right. I thought I was gracious! The truth is, I was scared my opinion would make them not like me. Especially if my opinion was "I don't like you." Sick, I know.

After a long time at it again, I started to break down. My people pleasing exhausted me, and my life, again, was unmanageable. It was at this time that my spirituality really began to mature. My spirit felt called to fast from church, to let go of what I thought that connection was supposed to look like, and trust my relationship with God. I was led on a life course that included words to learn, and to understand differently for different intervals of time. Words like: powerlessness, acceptance, responsibility, expectations, shame, confession, surrender, and forgiveness. Sometimes these words were around for weeks, sometimes months! It was a long spiritual trip that is, in fact, ongoing. Currently, the course is on replay, along with the word "follow." When I follow the Spirit of God that guides me, that heals me, that loves and cares for me, I generally do well by others and myself. I not only have more and greater things to give, but I have the freedom to do so without all the previous side effects.

I don't know that I would have known that it was God who saved me, had it not been for my path taking a turn through the church. God was with me all the while. God met me at my end, held me as I let go, and became the power to propel me forward. God shifted my confidence from myself to God's self. A few years ago, while praying, I was given a long crooked poem with one very clear stanza:

You are of substance
to which I hung your bones
to which I breathe My breath
and where My plans unfold.

I have worked at letting God be the source of my confidence. I have to breathe deep and let other people deal with their business. It is still hard for me to say no to people, even when I know it can be loving to do so. I have learned to take a good inventory of what is going on with me when I want to say "yes" to someone. Some days I am good at that, but I still struggle at times and find myself feeling trapped into "yesses" I wish I hadn't said. I try. I have reclaimed enough life that I can sense when I am full to give and when I am not. Even if I habitually say yes on accident, I have learned—as hard and humiliating as it may feel— that I can change my mind and say no. I have learned to feel the real motivation behind my "yes," and if I screw up, I can always start again.

This builds security in me, the kind of security that only comes from knowing you are held together by something greater than yourself, and trusting that that greater something is in charge of holding everyone else together as well.

THE HIDDEN DOORWAY TO EMPOWERMENT

AARON EDWARDS

"But now I am no longer the one acting—*I've lost control*—sin has taken up residence in me and *is wreaking havoc*."

—*Romans 7:17,* The Voice

I advocate for the empowerment of all people. I believe that when we can recognize our inherent value—see what God sees in us—we are on the path of healing and wholeness.

It almost sounds contradictory to then say I am also a huge proponent of our recognition of powerlessness. But it's not. It's just that powerlessness happens to be the hidden doorway to empowerment. It's the last place we think to look. It's also the last place we want to go. So we exhaust every other possibility, we look for a level of self-power that will catapult us into our empowerment. And it is only after we cannot find access within our own strength that we can start to feel like we are no longer in control.

I hear people say, "I'm just going to relinquish my control over this situation." Which, actually, is not completely accurate. We can't relinquish something we never had. The only thing we are giving up is our *illusion* of control. Which can feel just as terrifying as actually having had control. I have never seen anyone get to a place of powerlessness without feeling like they were thrust there against their will, even if they were the ones that created the circumstances surrounding their experience.

Usually, we can't get to our powerlessness with a simple conscious choice. It looks more like being dragged kicking and screaming then acknowledging what we have just been made painfully aware of: we do not have control.

When I am around people committed to their own recovery, it's easy to see that there's a certain knowledge in their eyes, an unspoken awareness that I don't see in very many other places. For them, the veil was lifted with step one. They saw behind the curtain that they themselves constructed to hide from the truth. But they didn't get there easily. It took (maybe literally) some blood, sweat, and tears. They had to get themselves to a place where they understood with absolute clarity that their best efforts were not going to get them out of the hole they had dug themselves into.

I once heard an alcoholic with thirty years sobriety say, "Thank God for alcohol." Alcohol was simply the vehicle he used to learn something that he would not have believed to be true otherwise: his own powerlessness over his life. Obviously, alcoholism is not the only path to powerlessness.

When I first began pastoral counseling, I saw a common theme emerge. Some would tell me about marriage difficulties or parenting difficulties or job difficulties. Sometimes they would feel better just having the space to talk about it. I listened and encouraged and told them about the hope found in Christ. But they were mostly looking for a strategic way out of the difficulty. We would find ways to cope with what was happening, and they would walk away feeling a little bit better. Rinse, and repeat until the next week. The cycle started to feel taxing for me, and them.

Peppered in between were people with various impossible situations. People whose addiction had become beyond unmanageable. People whose marriage had become beyond repair. People who no longer had job difficulties; they had no jobs and no job prospects. People that no longer had a difficult relationship with their children, but no relationship with their children at all. People who had lost a child.

The common thing that I saw emerge was that people with varying degrees of difficulties seemed to manage themselves from week to week without too much progression or digression. But for the ones whose lives had become unmanageable, impossible, there was a sacred space created for breakthrough! This was possible because the illusion of control was seen as just that: an illusion. Their powerlessness led them to surrender, which then led to a spiritual empowerment that they could have never produced by their own management.

This is the truth of the gospel and the upside-down kingdom. We all want to see the miracle; we just don't want to *need* the miracle. We cheer when we see Jesus heal the leper, but God forbid if we actually *were* the leper. We are not going to see the miracle until we recognize our need for it. We are the leper. Thank God!

LET GO AND LET GOD

DALE RYAN

A couple of years ago I fell and broke my leg. When we got to the hospital, the doctor said, "Well, your leg is broken in three places. It's a fairly common pattern. I'll make some recommendations based on what has worked for other people who have had this kind of problem, and then you can decide what you want to do." I didn't need to think for very long. What was there to think about? Just fix it! If the suggestions worked for other people, then that was all I needed to know. It did not occur to me to ask if it was biblical to put screws in your leg to hold some of the bones together. I didn't ask whether there was any spiritual significance to the doctor's suggested steps. I just thought, "Well, this seems to work for other folks, so let's give it a try."

But what if we go to a Twelve Step program, or to a counselor, and we hear, "The trouble you're having is a fairly common pattern. I'll make some recommendations based on what has worked for other people who have had this kind of problem, and then you can decide what to do"? Well, things are a little more complicated for us. It does occur to many of us to ask, "Are these suggested steps consistent with the Bible?" This is an important question. Recovery is not like putting screws in your leg to fix a broken bone. Recovery is about spiritual change. For that reason it is perfectly legitimate for us to ask whether it is consistent with the spiritual resources we trust—and for many of us that includes the Bible.

So here's a key question that we need to think about: are the basic principles of recovery consistent with the principles we find in the Bible? My own conviction is that they are. It was from the Bible, for example, that the founders of Alcoholics Anonymous learned the principles that were structured into the Twelve Steps. This is much too short of an article to look at all the fundamental principles of recovery and the biblical foundations for each of them, but we have space to look closely at one principle as an example of the connections between the Bible and basic recovery principles. Are the connections thin? With only a verse here and there that might apply? Or is the connection a significant one?

The principle I would like to look at is captured well in the commonly heard slogan "Let go and let God." The principle is this: recovery is not just something that we do. **Recovery is something that God does for us and in us.** It is something we receive from God. We let go of our attempts to do what we cannot do by ourselves and let God do what needs to be done. We receive the healing, growth, and serenity that God longs to give us.

Unfortunately, receiving is not something that most of us are particularly good at. I've been watching my grandson recently. Receiving seems to come easy for him. If you give him a present in a box, it is like giving him two presents—there's the box, and then there's the present in the box. You give him something and he just lights up with eagerness and enthusiasm. Somewhere between early childhood and adulthood, however, most of us lose that. We don't receive like that anymore. That eagerness and enthusiasm are replaced by other things. If someone gives something to us, we may find ourselves thinking, "Does this mean I am obligated to give something in return?" or, "Is this some kind of attempt to control my behavior?" Or maybe we just respond with, "No, you shouldn't, really. There's somebody that needs this more than me. I should be giving you things." By adulthood, most of us have acquired many layers of resistance to receiving.

I don't think the Christian community as it exists today helps us very much here. I have spent most of my life in churches that emphasize that the very beginning of the Christian life is about receiving—receiving salvation—but from day two on, the focus tends to be on giving. We get locked into a giving-priority mode very quickly. Now, there is nothing wrong with giving. It is clearly good to give. But what "Let go and let God" suggests is that there is a kind of spiritual priority to receiving. In part, this is because receiving is a necessary prerequisite to giving. You can't give away what you haven't received, at least not without very significant negative consequences. Let's look at the biblical evidence for the spiritual priority of receiving.

The Bible begins with an account of Creation. What is the main point of the biblical account of Creation? It is a description of the basic structure of existence on this planet. Life on this planet works like this: God gives life; we receive life. It's also very clear that God not only gave life and we received it, but that God *continually* gives life and we *continually* receive it. The Creator didn't stop being the Creator after He created. God is still the Creator. God is still giving life, and we are still receiving life. None of us can guarantee the next beat of our heart. We cannot guarantee we will be alive at the end of the hour. Every beat of our heart is a gift from the Creator God. It is a gift of love and grace to you and me. It's very hard to stay in conscious contact with the fact of this gift as we live through a day. Somehow, it is too much to pay attention to, but it is the most fundamental truth, which we find at the very beginning of the Bible. God is giving life to us all day long, and our task is to receive—to let go of our anxious attempts to be the author of our own lives and to let God give our life to us.

Now let's fast-forward to Abraham. God comes out of nowhere to Abraham and says, "I'm going to give to you. I'm going to give you a land. I'm going to give you lots of children. And I'm going to give you the role of being a blessing." Notice that God comes to Abraham and insists on being the one who gives. God says, "I'm going to give to you." God gives. Abraham receives. It is important to remember that Abraham's world was a very religious world. There were all kinds of religious faiths in the ancient world, but the dominant instinct of all those religions was that it was our responsibility to give to God. Maybe God was hungry and our job was to give God food. Maybe God was angry and we needed to give him something so he wouldn't be so angry. The only religious instinct available in Abraham's world was that people were supposed to give to God. So it must have been a real shock to have God come and say just the opposite. Nothing in Abraham's world could have prepared him to understand this God-who-gives. It turned his world upside down. How can you serve a God-who-gives when the only God you have ever known is a God-who-needs-to-receive?

It is clear in the biblical text that Abraham doesn't get it right away.

He is a bit slow, Abraham. God says to him, "I'm going to give you land. I'm going to give you lots of kids. I'm going to make you to be a blessing." There is stuff here for Abraham to do—the arrangement is not about Abraham being passive. God is giving Abraham land, so Abraham needs to go to the land. I probably do not need to explain what Abraham has to do to have lots of kids, but he has to be a consistent husband and father. And Abraham has to go about the business of being a blessing. God is going to give Abraham land, children, and blessings, but Abraham needs to go to the land, have lots of kids, and do whatever it takes so that all his neighbors, after a period of time, will say to him: "You know, it's a blessing to have you in the neighborhood. We're all better off having you here." That's God's plan.

Abraham has a different plan. He doesn't understand the God-who-gives. So Abraham devises his own alternative: plan B. God's plan A was to go to the land, Abraham's plan B is to go to Egypt. Bad choice. God's plan A was to have lots of kids, Abraham's plan B is to give his wife to the Egyptian Pharaoh. God's plan for Abraham was to make him a blessing, but before long, the Pharaoh is tired of Abraham's lies and throws him out. Abraham gets it all wrong. He wants to be in control; he wants to be in charge; he thinks he is smart enough, good enough, clever enough to make it all work. Like many of us, he doesn't want to be the one to receive.

Let's fast forward to a much later point. Gideon is a military commander during a time when the tribes of Israel are a loose confederation. There is a military threat from the east, and Gideon puts together an army of thirty-two thousand men. For the time, this is enough for a "shock and awe" strategy. Gideon comes to God after raising this big army, and says, "I think we can give You the victory."

God says, "This does not feel right to me—*you* giving *me* the victory. *I* want to give *you* the victory. If you go out with this army and win, people will say that you had the power and the state-of-the-art military hardware, and you won because you were stronger than the other guy." God says, "I'm going to feel much more comfortable about this if you send a bunch of these people home and fight this battle with a less impressive military force."

So Gideon sends half of his men home. There are two or three cycles of this as God keeps telling Gideon to send people home. Finally, Gideon comes to God and says something like, "I do not think that I can give You the victory." And God says, "Perfect. I think we're ready to get something done."

The principle is clear enough. We can try to do recovery out of our own strength. We can raise up an army of thirty-two thousand men. We can go to battle. But it doesn't work very well. I don't know how many of you have tried to stay sober by just doing sobriety instead of receiving sobriety, but it's a hard path. I've known people who have been able to walk that path for some period of time, but they often just get tired and grouchy. The quality of the sobriety suffers, because in order to do your own recovery, you have to work hard, and work harder, and work your hardest, and eventually you get very tired. That's what would have been Gideon's fate if God hadn't come to him and said, "We're going to have to do this from a position of weakness or I just don't know how I can help you."

The good news is that God can do for us what we can't really do for ourselves. But there is some bad news. In Gideon's story you certainly get a sense of the terror that comes with being the people whose job it is to receive. Our part in God's plan can be pretty scary. It means going out against an enemy who we know we cannot beat on our own strength. We will be afraid. We will feel vulnerable. We will ask, "How is this going to work if I can't make it work? How is this going to happen if I'm not powerful enough to make it happen?" Some of the scariest work we do in the recovery process is facing our weaknesses, bringing them to God, and being shocked again and again by God's insistence that it is precisely our weaknesses that make it possible for God to do what needs to be done.

Let's fast forward to Jesus, who put this very simply: "All you who labor and are burdened, I will give you rest."

"I'll give," he says. "You receive." You will find rest for your soul. What is rest for the soul? If we didn't have the word serenity, we might decide to call it soul-rest. God wants to give us that. "I'll give you soul-rest," Jesus says. When Jesus taught His disciples how to pray, he said, "Give us this day." You, God, You be the one to give. We will be the ones to receive.

You see this emphasis repeatedly in Jesus's teachings. Let's look at one parable. If you take an introductory course on parables, one of the first things you'll learn is that parables tend to have one point. They are rarely five-point sermons. With the parable of the waiting father, unfortunately, people often focus on only part of the story. They talk only about the prodigal son, who left and spent all his money on cocaine and prostitutes—that's just my guess about how he spent his money, but it's probably not a bad guess. But there are two sons. So what is the one point that is the same for both sons? What do these two sons have in common? The younger son went off and spent all his money on drugs and prostitutes, and the other stayed home acquiring a bunch of resentments. In that sense, they are quite different. But what do they have in common? The text is very clear about this. Both of these sons have essentially the same strategy for how they are going to be a part of the father's family.

What is the prodigal son's strategy? In the parable we see him walking home, practicing his speech. He is going to say to his father, "I will be your servant." That's his strategy for how to get back into the father's family. He will be a servant. What does a servant do? A servant gives and gives and gives. If a servant stops giving—well, that's a big problem. So what happens? When the son gets home, he doesn't even get his whole speech out before the father says, "That's not the deal. I'm the one who gives. You be the one who receives." And the father proceeds to give. This must have been profoundly confusing to this young man, who was convinced that the only way to get back in the good graces of his father was to give.

Now, what is the older son's strategy? When it becomes apparent that the older son has some resentments, his father has a conversation with him. The older brother says, "I have served you all this time, and now my brother is the one getting honored. It doesn't seem right." So the older son has the same basic strategy as the younger son: he thinks he gets to be part of the father's family because he is giving so much—serving so much. Yet the father says to him, "Everything I have is yours. I am the one who gives. Your job is to be the one who receives."

What do both sons need? They need to learn to receive from their gracious father. They need to let go of their plans of earning their keep by being "good enough" givers, and they need to let their father love them. The spiritual principle is very clear: Let go and let God.

Let's fast forward to the early church. The Christian church doesn't have a golden age. We don't look back to a time when everything was just the way it was supposed to be. If you read the New Testament, you'll find very troubled, broken people trying to find some way to be faithful to Jesus. In Paul's letters, you find that one of the things that started to go wrong in the very beginning of the church was that people really wanted the Christian life to be about being right. They wanted the movement to be about us being good people who give to God. Paul keeps coming back to this idea in a variety of ways, saying, "That's not the deal. Not even close. God gives. We receive. It's about grace." And what does grace look like? It is always a narrative about a God who gives and gives and gives, and about a people who receive and receive and receive.

Now, I know that some people will experience this emphasis on receiving as unbalanced—that giving must have its place. Let me just suggest that if you want to balance this teaching with an emphasis on giving to God, you start by giving to God the things God has asked for. Give God your burdens. Consider Jesus's clear teaching on this: "Come to me, all you who are weary and burdened, and I will give you rest. Take my yoke upon you and learn from me, for I am gentle and humble in heart, and you will find rest for your souls. For my yoke is easy and my burden is light" (Matthew 11:28-30).

If your spiritual life is about you doing the heavy lifting, something has gone very wrong. Paul is equally clear about this. He saw Christians who started their spiritual journey by receiving grace from God, but then got caught up in a being-good-enough, trying-hard-enough, being-dedicated-enough kind of faith, and he warned them about all such performance-based spiritualties: "Stand firm, then, and do not let yourselves be burdened again by a yoke of slavery" (Galatians 5:1).

Nothing is more debilitating to our spiritual lives than the illusion that we are in charge and in control, or that we are the ones who are going to make this work. All that this kind of spirituality does for us is make us burdened and tired.

Another biblical theme that makes the same point is the theme of God feeding His people. If you are hungry, if you are thirsty, God wants to feed you. I don't think that this comes instinctively to us. I do think the Judeo-Christian religion is unique in the history of world religions in having a God that feeds His people. Most religious instinct in the history of our species has been that we need to feed God.

Think about God's provision of manna in the wilderness. Think about God setting a table for us in the presence of our enemies. Think about the loaves and fishes. Think of the Eucharist—God feeding us with spiritual food. God loves to feed His people. God loves to give nourishment to us. Our task is to receive.

Since I started with the first chapter of Genesis, maybe I should end with the last chapter of Revelation. In most English translations, the book of Revelation ends with a section that does not appear in the best early manuscripts. The original ending appears to be Revelation 22:17: "Let the one who is thirsty come; and let the one who wishes take the free gift of the water of life."

The best one-word description I can think of for people who are impacted by the addictive process is thirsty. We are thirsty people—people to whom God wants to give, freely, the water of life. Is this too good to be true? It might feel like that at times. We might resist it for this reason, among many others. But God is a patient God. From the beginning of the Bible to the very end, you get a clear and consistent image of God. God wants to be the One-Who-Gives. The invitation is still there: come and drink.

May God grant you the courage, wisdom, and strength you need
to receive the free gift of the water of life.

POWERLESSNESS

MATT RUSSELL

Powerless. Who likes to admit that we are powerless? I mean, you and me, we sturdy ourselves against life. We amass our resources, protect ourselves, and head out into the world with all we can muster. *Every natural instinct cries out against the idea of personal powerlessness.* But in an instant, it can all change. Powerlessness has a thousand faces and a million expressions. At its core it's about life we cannot control, about reality we cannot shape, about a future we cannot master. It's a mother holding her infant in the emergency room with a 104-degree temperature, realizing that there is nothing she can do to make her baby well. It's a phone call from your doctor to tell you your test results have returned and you have cancer. It's the feeling that you don't have control over how much alcohol you drink, how many drugs you use, how much and what you eat, your sexual urges or your shopping impulses. It's the feeling of unworthiness and shame that washes over in an instant, or the onset of anxiety, depression, or dread that comes on like the flu, seemingly out of nowhere. Powerlessness rears its head in how we spend our money, how we spend our time, how people act and react toward us. A friend of mine in the program said it well:

> For me, powerlessness has one name, and that is reality. The longer I am on this planet the more I realize how little power I have. Life is, and life will do what life will do. I think I can pray, accept, love, and notice, but I don't have a lot of power. My lack of acceptance and power has caused me a lot of pain and misery. I have come to believe that only through surrender do I live a life that makes sense. When I deny my powerlessness I can hurt a lot of people by insulating myself from the truth. I have spent a lot of time trying

to control the people in my life by helping them. I now realize that I cannot help anyone; I can just let them be themselves. I am truly powerless over life. I spent a lot of time believing that I am in control of things, but it is all just my illusions.

A lot of us can relate to this. We've invested in the Western illusion that we have access to all the power we need to be self-sufficient, self-aware, self-actualized, and self-made. This is an illusion that causes pain and misery for us and those around us. When we confront experiences of powerlessness, there is a temptation to believe that powerlessness is something we can overcome or manage our way out of. Is this the headwaters of denial? Is this where our self-deception takes root? Is this the gap between the reality that we want to create and project, and the reality of our present situation? In this way, denial gets played out in our lives like a Monty Python scene I remember. When King Arthur meets the Black Knight, having cartoonishly and literally dismantled him, the knight, his limbs laying on the ground, says, "Tis merely a flesh wound—come back!—I'll bite your knee caps!"

Denial protects our psyche from having to face the reality of what we have lost, what our addiction and behaviors are costing us. The temptation in our culture is to believe that powerlessness is a stage that we can move through with our own resources, maybe even with the resources of God. We think of powerlessness as a stage of development, rather than a state of life's reality. It is not something we pass through or grow out of on the way to the American dream. Our Christian faith and the Program point to another reality, another path, an alternative truth, and it is this: powerlessness is at the heart of our humanity and is the entrance to transformation. For many of us, it takes a long time to walk through this threshold, and it is usually great pain that carries us beyond the borders of our own control.

I remember the first time I ever felt powerless. I was fourteen years old and my mother (an alive and vivacious woman) started to have unexplained seizures and other physical problems due to cancer in her brain that would go undiscovered for another six years. I remember coming home one day and finding my sister in a panic; the concoction of anti-seizure medication that my mother was prescribed had risen to a toxic level and my mom was having difficulty breathing. My sister, just sixteen years old, insisted that we take her to the emergency room, so we put my mom in the car and started driving. I was in the backseat with my mom when she started to seize and then completely stopped breathing. I had to work to keep her breathing as we drove down the interstate to the hospital. As a teenager, I was utterly overwhelmed, powerless to save my mother. I felt like she was going to die in my arms in the back of that car. She didn't die that day, but I remember lying awake in my bed that night swearing that I would never feel that depth of desperation, fear, or terror ever again. I vowed that I would never descend into powerlessness like that again. That is the day I became an addict. Now, it was a few years before I found the right drug, the right process, the perfect behavior that insulated me, but I tell you that night, alone in my bed, I shook my fist at the universe and promised never to feel that small again. It was just a matter of time.

The river that runs underneath powerlessness is fear. The fear of being destroyed, of being insignificant, of not being or having enough. The fear of being rejected, of not being in control, of being left. The fear of dying, the fear of shame. The fear of being extinguished or overcome, and finally, overwhelmed.

Enter addiction. Addiction is the complex behaviors and patterns of thinking that we employ to protect us from debilitating fear. And addiction works—it numbs us, distracts us, and displaces our attention. We create smoke screens and symptoms and get lost in the haze (literally) of it all. The difficulty of admitting powerlessness comes when the structure of our whole existence is defined by avoiding this reality. Many of us, feeling cornered, desperate, and at the end of our rope, construct a complex pattern of excuses and self-talk:

I can quit anytime. I've got a handle on this.
It's not that bad. Losing that job was not my fault.
It's really his/her fault.
If she/he did _____, I wouldn't do _____.
I will quit working so much when the kids get older.

I will only drink every other day.
This is the last time.

We minimize our behavior, the places we go, the behaviors we hide, and the fears that we live with. Ultimately, this self-deception costs us our intimacy with ourselves, with God, and with other people. We feel so small, exposed, angry, and hurt. At some point in our lives, many of us just resign to managing the pain and the mess. It's scary to think that we can become so good at this that we might live in the shadow land of addiction for the rest of our lives.

The question Jesus asks the crippled man echoes in our desire to be free from the prison of addiction. For thirty-eight years, a man lay by the pool of Bethesda waiting for the waters to be stirred in order to enter the pools to be healed. Jesus comes to him and asks him a simple question: "Do you want to be made whole?" (John 5:6)

Underneath our addiction is a desire to be whole, complete, and free, and Jesus knows this. This question is inescapable for us: *do you want to be made whole?* The truth is that we become dependent upon our anxieties, addictions, and regret, and they become, as Christian Wiman says:

". . . useful to us, whether as explanations for a life that never quite finds its true force or direction, or as fuel for ambition, or as a kind of reflexive secular religion that, paradoxically, unites us with others in a shared sense of complete isolation: you feel at home in the world only by never feeling at home in the world."

And so the question of "wholeness" stands at the threshold of our redemption. Wholeness and powerlessness are partners in the journey of redemption, and because Jesus knows this, He asks us: *"Do you want to be made whole?"*

It was the persistence of questions like this in my life that helped me realize that I am at the bottom, that I am the crippled man on the side of a pool, able to see a different life but so powerless, ineffective, and screwed up to move in that direction. And surprisingly, this was the entrance and invitation into the life of God. This was falling into the arms of God, the beginning of letting go, of taking "one day at a time." What a great paradox this is! Our powerlessness, despair, inability, and shame become an invitation, a hallway, a window, a door, a crack that opens into the life of God. Over and over in the gospels, Jesus expresses this alternative reality: "For whoever wants to save their life will lose it, but whoever loses their life for me will find it" (Matthew 16:25).

And it was here, amidst all the insulation of my behaviors, that I heard the whisper of God, felt the presence of God in my deepest shadow. God did not abandon me in my youth in the back seat of that car with my dying mother; He held me as I held my mother. I began to understand that God was there in solidarity with me, that He had not left me, and that very place of powerlessness became the seed of "belief." Not rational assent to statements of doctrine, but experience of love that is self-authenticating and irrefutably deep. God was with me, and it was my powerlessness and all the darkness that fueled it that opened the door.

In *Messy Spirituality*, Mike Yacconelli says this way of faith is anything but a straight line. Faith is anything but tidy and neat because you and I are anything but tidy and neat. He says that the spiritual life birthed from our powerlessness is not a formula and it is not a test. It is a relationship. Spirituality at its core is not about competency, but intimacy. Spirituality is not about perfection, but connection. That is why the entrance into the spiritual life starts with facing the reality of myself everyday. If we are invested in holding on to our own power, we will never hold on to the divine power available to us. That is why powerlessness is the entrance: within powerlessness we step back from our compulsiveness and attachments, and stand in what Richard Rohr calls "the naked now." It is within this place that the love of God, the fellowship of recovery rooms, and Christian community begin to clothe us in the divine reality of our identity: we are loved, and nothing can separate us from the love of God.

I AM STILL HERE

KELLY HALL

To the blind eye, the deaf ear,
the turned face, and the fallen head;
To the tense neck, the burdened shoulder,
the hard, broken heart, and the breath-less lung;
To the pointing finger, the stealing hand,
and the long arm reaching for the law;
To the ever-marching leg,
the tired, wayward foot, and the banged toe—

I am still here.
Right here with all that I AM,
giving.
Take on My sight as yours;
hear My voice, wear My anointing.
Relax beneath My mantle,
let Me awaken you to live!

Surrender your way, give Me a try—
I am not asking you to be mindless,
but mindful.
I will handle the things you cannot change;
I will teach you acceptance
and send you out to change the things you can.
Lean into My wisdom,
allow Me to be the difference.

Surrender

CURRICULUM

KIM V. ENGELMANN

"Whoever finds their life will lose it, and whoever loses their life for my sake will find it." —*Matthew 10:39*

THEOLOGICAL IMPLICATIONS

In listening to the surrender clip, the irony that creeps into all of the testimonials is the simple fact that what we are being asked to surrender in our recovery process is ultimately not anything worth keeping to begin with. We cling to what we know and what is familiar because, in a world of uncertainty, even destructive old patterns die hard. The fantasy that our self-sufficiency and false persona will somehow fulfill us assumes that something unreal can offer sustenance and fulfillment to the pervasive longings of our hearts for God. The paradox of surrender is that in letting go of what is not real, we encounter the One who is eternally true and completely authentic. In surrender, because we have let go of the lie of self-sufficiency, there now exists within us space and opportunity for the wealth of God's eternal love to infuse our heart.

QUESTIONS FOR REFLECTION

Do you think that surrender is a one-time experience or an ongoing life journey? Or both?

Do you remember a time when you surrendered something to God? How did you get to the point of wanting to surrender? How did you know that surrender had actually happened?

Sometimes people resist surrendering to God because they think it might mean that their sense of who they are would get violated, or that they might become a doormat for the world. How would you explain surrender to someone who has this kind of perspective?

In your experience, what is the hardest part of surrender? The best part?

Why is surrender so necessary for recovery?

PRAYER

As I walk with You, I pray that I would not see You as a God who wants to take things away from me. Rather help me to "get" that You have always been for me. In asking me to surrender, You are asking me to give You all of the stuff that is corrosive in my life so that there will be space inside of me for Your life-giving presence. Come, Holy Spirit, and help me to let go of the lies so that I can embrace the truth of Your goodness. In Jesus's name, Amen.

WRITE YOUR OWN PRAYER:

A BLESSING FOR THE CONTEMPLATION OF SURRENDER

KELLY HALL

To You, the I Am,
I come as I am, with my many faces.
I come empty handed, clutching to my "things."
I come behind walls; I come with resistance.
I come wanting to be changed, but hoping if nothing else…
to be accepted, to know wholeness.
I am willing to be willing
to be healed as You please, to be liberated on and on.
I give up my control, I surrender,
At least I surrender my "right now."
Holy Spirit, reach back to me,
restore me, grow me, and remind me You never leave.
Help me see the blessing of being
who I am right where I am.
Help me grow into who You imagined.

Help me come further into You than I ever dreamed.

ALL OR NOTHING

TAYLOR GAHM

I have heard quite a few Christians say that God wants to "have all of me." Sometimes it's said in such a way I am left feeling that if I'm not willing to give God all of me, then He doesn't want any of me. But what if God really is in love with me and is willing to take what He can get? What if He will stop at nothing to get what He wants and in so doing will even take the seconds, the scraps, and the leftovers?

Because a god who wants all or nothing sounds like a god who has never been in love before.

But a God that will take what He can get is blinded by love and has a plan for me that He has no intention of messing up, regardless of how much I do or don't give Him. This God doesn't need me to prove anything to Him. He wants to give, not take. Perhaps if I want to experience the good things He has for me, I might need to make a little room in my hands so I can receive them.

Maybe I need to let go of whatever I'm hanging on to.

The God I have experienced is in it for the long haul. He doesn't require that I be willing to give Him everything all at once. He is far less concerned about what I can give Him than He is about what He wants to give me. Because this God is in love with me. He isn't trying to trick me or ask me to prove that I'm worth loving.

He just loves me. He loves all of us. And He says we're enough.

He goes to great lengths to show me that there's nothing I need to do or think or believe to deserve or be worthy of such ridiculousness. So maybe I just need to learn to let go. Maybe we all need to just let go.

Jesus (to His disciples): "If you want to follow Me, you must deny your-self *the things you think you want*. You must pick up your cross and follow Me. The person who wants to save his life must lose it, and she who loses her life for Me will find it."

—Matthew 16:24-25

"Sometimes you fall into the hands of a loving God. Sinners falling into the hands of a loving, graceful, tender-hearted, slow-to-anger God will change one's life forever."

—Dale Ryan

GOD, AS WE UNDERSTOOD HIM

JAMES RYAN
EDITED BY ANDREW MARTIN

At the time of my spiritual awakening I was six months dry in a little room above a drugstore in the hills of western Maine. I spent those days wandering the streets in solitude, talking to myself. I worked in a little shack behind a gas station where I counted the empty cans that people brought in for redemption. The customers that approached my shack would hear a lively conversation going on within. Then they'd find me in there, wild-eyed and alone.

Six months dry wasn't much fun. It was like having an itch in my head I couldn't scratch, and that itch gave me weird ideas. I thought everyone was looking at me all the time, talking about me or thinking bad things. I heard scratching on the walls of my room at night, scratching that wouldn't go away until I drew a crucifix on the wall in just the right spot. I also had the idea that I was on the fast track to literary greatness. People didn't appreciate me, not yet, and I was going to show them. I was designing a novel machine on the walls of my studio apartment. Plastic sheets with markings in black ink and an elaborate system of sticky notes and yarn decorated my living space. Dominoes and dice scattered around the floor were the key to the whole system, although I'm not sure I could have explained that system to anyone if I'd had the chance. Nevertheless, I was going to show all the jerks that ever hurt me. They'd be sorry they were cruel to me when I was winking at the Queen of Sweden and accepting the Nobel Prize.

That's how it was with me when I went dry for a while. I'd get sober. I'd go to meetings. I'd slowly lose my grip on reality.

"Keep coming back," they'd tell me. And I would for a while, but how long can a man go to meetings when he's busy pretending he's a genius and avoiding all those phantom people who want to creep into his mind?

Anyway, meetings didn't seem to offer much. You'd steal down into some church basement and take a chair in a roomful of people just as crazy as you, and then they'd all start talking. Some would bitch about their lives, some would tell stories about getting drunk and high, some would talk real loud about God, and some would do what I did—they'd drink up the coffee and shift around in their seats nervously until it was time to go. It was all a waste of time, really, except for the free coffee. "If you want what we've got..." they said, but I never wanted anything anybody in those rooms had. The people who were sober the longest were more miserable than I was, so who needs it?

The worst meetings were the ones where they talked about God. I'd heard plenty of God-talk when I was growing up Baptist, and I sure as hellfire did not need some long-winded, self-righteous drunk to remind me of all that crap. It made me mad. So I stayed away from those meetings. Sometimes, after hearing somebody preach at a meeting, I'd stay away from meetings altogether for a while.

My pattern was to bounce in and out. I'd be "in the program" for a few months, and then I'd get sick of people and go it alone. When the isolation got to be too much, I'd drop in on some other meetings for a while. By bouncing in and out, I could put as much as a few years of sobriety together without having to really be one of those sad-sack has-beens whining their lives away anonymously in four-dollar chairs.

But then something happened to me when I was living in Maine. It was a fairly ordinary something, the kind of thing that happens to people all the time—sober, high, or otherwise—but when it happened to me, things started to change in my life.

As it happened, I had a girlfriend. In the state I was in, there weren't too many women that would have me, but I somehow managed to find one and we had our way with each other for a few weeks. Then, on my birthday, it happened. She dumped me. Two weeks into our "relationship," she figured out that I was too desperate, insane, and needy to make a good boyfriend, and she let me know.

Now break-ups happen all the time. I'd lost a number of women in and out of sobriety, so this was nothing new. Maybe it was the fact that it was my birthday that gave that break-up a special punch, or maybe I was finally getting tired of being such a freak. The truth was I didn't really know how to be a human being. I was giving it my best shot, but I always seemed to end up all itchy and irritable and uncomfortable in my own skin. In order to get by in life I needed to have something around me to take the edge off. Weed worked. Beer worked. So did a number of other drugs. But when I was staying dry, I needed something else to get me through the day, and I liked a woman for that. A woman, when she has the mind to do it, can make a man feel satisfied. So when I could get with someone, I did.

When women dumped me, I was thrown back into my solitude. I had to scratch my own itches again. I had to go back to pretending to be human while feeling all the time like an inhuman creep. Break-ups were never any fun for me, but after this particular break-up, I was given a special grace—I got to take a hard look at my life.

Did I have anything left that was going to make my life amount to anything?

No.

Was there anything at all that could distract me from myself and my pain for any considerable amount of time?

No.

Could I think of anything that I hadn't tried yet to make myself feel okay?

No, I could not.

I'd tried everything I could think of to make myself function as a proper example of *Homo sapiens*, and none of it worked. Drugs made me crazy. Not using drugs made me crazy. Meetings made me sick to my stomach. Rehabs were fun for a while, but then you had to go back to the real world again. The nut house was the same way; you could have a good time there, and then they'd throw you out on your ass. I'd climbed mountains and read books. I'd lived in five different states and two foreign countries. I'd seen pill doctors and "talk therapy" doctors. I'd sat alone in the corner of hipster coffee shops and filled journal after journal with sad notes about myself.

None of it worked.

After she broke up with me, I cried for a while. Then I left my house and went down to a meeting I'd heard about from this guy I'd met through a mutual friend. I didn't go expecting to find anything useful, I just went because I didn't know what to do with myself. I was in pain, so I had to have a way to kill some time.

That's where I was spiritually on the night that I first met the Living Spirit. I was a sad, self-piteous, half-crazy jerk showing up at a meeting just to kill some time.

The meeting started like most others—there were a few readings, people said some prayers—then the chairperson started reading out of a book. He read a while and then talked about what he'd read. When he was done talking, he paused to see if anyone else wanted to speak. As it turned out, someone did want to speak, and she went on for a while about something she liked in the reading. Someone else picked up the conversation after her, and so on.

I can't quote you verbatim what was said that night, but I can tell you that it was a message unlike any that I had ever heard in five years of hopping in and out of meetings from state to state. Anywhere I ever went—AA, NA, whatever—the people spoke about their lives as addicts and how happy they were that they didn't have to drink or use that day. Sometimes they spoke about their daily struggles with staying clean and sober, and the message usually boiled down to something like this: "My life sucks, but I didn't get high over it." That was the sort of thing people "in the program" called "strength and hope."

At this meeting, the message was different. They weren't talking about how much their lives sucked when they were using, they spoke about the pain and chaos they used to live in when they were dry for a while without a spiritual experience. They described the restlessness, the paranoia, the sleepless nights. They spoke about the trail of broken relationships and the jobs they left behind them every time they went on·a "dry bender." (One man had lost his wife when he was two years clean in NA.) Several people voiced the opinion that they were more pleasant to be around high than dry.

They told "war stories," not about the using days—although they had plenty of those as well—but about the days of bare abstinence when all they did was show up at meetings and talk.

The stories these people told were the stories of my life, life as I was living it right then. When one man described his daily affairs when he lacked a spiritual experience, I was convinced that he had been following me around and taking notes. How did these people know so much about me? How could they describe the inner workings of my mind? Clearly, they were not suffering from the symptoms they described. Their eyes were clear, and they could laugh about things that were still terribly painful for me, sensitive guy that I was.

These people also spoke about God. A lot. I hadn't heard so much God-talk since I was in a youth-group Bible study. It made my skin crawl, and yet I could tell there was something different about these folks. They weren't just banging on a pulpit and talking out the side of their necks. They knew what it was like to suffer, but they were no longer suffering. They had a real solution to the problem of addiction—high or dry. Not only that, but they had a different way of talking about God.

As far as I knew then, most people who talked about God had an agenda. They wanted you to sign off on a set of doctrines and were willing to bully and intimidate you with hellfire threats if it would bring you on board. These people, though—these drunks and junkies and Alanons—they didn't seem to have anything to sell. "You can think whatever you want about God," they said. "God's not an idea; God is a living power." "This isn't about what you believe; it's about what you do." "Just throw out everything you think you know about God and start over."

They said stuff like that, and they meant it. Not only were they serious about the God-stuff, but they were demonstrating through their testimonies that something had radically changed their lives, and that something had to be beyond human power. They were like me—they'd tried everything else they could think of before they turned to God, and nothing else ever worked.

The meeting left me terribly rattled. They pushed my "God button" pretty hard and I was sore about it. I wanted to tell them all to screw and never go back again, but I couldn't get up the nerve. The feeling in that room haunted me. These were real people who really had an answer to the problems that were bugging me. They had something that I'd never seen anywhere else in the fellowships. They had what I wanted.

So I went back.

I went back and I kept going back. That guy who told me about the meeting eventually became my sponsor and he put me to work on the Twelve Steps, and the Twelve Steps pushed my "God button" all over again.

If you've ever read the Steps, you know what's going on at the heart of this program. There's a lot of talk in meetings about "taking what works and leaving the rest," but when you read the Steps you know— this program is about God all the way through. In the past, I'd always read the Steps and skipped over the God stuff because I felt that I could leave out the parts I wasn't interested in.

The trouble with that approach is that when you take the God stuff out, there's not much program left. You can't get past Step Two without having to believe. So if you really try to work the Steps without God, you end up living a powerless, unmanageable life, sitting in those meetings in a world of hurt, and just barely staying dry.

When my new sponsor started working me through the Steps, he didn't soft-pedal the God stuff at all. Either I was going to come to terms with my resentment toward God, or this program wasn't going to work. A doorknob or a roomful of drunks was not going to fit the bill either. I had to let real, live Spiritual Power into my life so that it could make some necessary changes. Furthermore, I didn't get to have any say over what this Power did or did not change. I couldn't hold on to anything. God was going to have it all, and God could do whatever He wanted with me. My job was just to let go and get out of the way.

For a guy that's actively resentful of his Christian upbringing, the idea of surrender is a hard pill to swallow. I hated the very idea of God, so how was I supposed to be willing to let God take over everything in my life? Fortunately, Step Three was carefully worded for hard cases like me. I didn't have to turn my life over to "Jesus" or "Buddha" or "Allah." I had to turn it over to "God, as we understood Him."

As adamant as my sponsor was about the fact that I had to give up everything to this invisible Spirit that I didn't believe in, he was equally willing to let me believe whatever I wanted about that Spirit. In fact, I didn't even have to believe in God at all.

"You don't have to believe in God," he said, "you just have to give Him a try."

Give Him a try. That was new. I could bring all my resentment and doubts to the table, I didn't have to sign off on any statement of faith, and I could still have a shot at having one of those spiritual experiences these guys kept talking about. After I had my own spiritual experience, I could make up my own mind, and nobody was going to tell me any different. If God didn't exist or couldn't help me, then I hadn't lost anything on the deal. I could go back to my miserable life knowing that I'd at least given this a try. That phrase—God, as we understood Him—meant that I was granted total intellectual freedom in the realm of faith. The only catch was that I would have to give God everything I had—my personality, my future, my interests, my beliefs—and let this Power reshape them as it saw fit.

When my sponsor saw that I understood the terms of my surrender, he gave me a week to think about it. "Spend some time with this," he said. "Don't take it lightly."

Lightly? I took it darned seriously. Was I really going to get down on my knees and hold this guy's hands and tell God He could have me? I was afraid I'd just be making a total ass out of myself. It wasn't going to work anyway, right? So why even bother? What was I even thinking by hanging out with these people? I struggled with doubts and reservations for the next five days, and then I had my first experience with the Power that hangs around AA.

It was the end of autumn and I was stir-crazy, so I went out for an evening stroll. I headed for the library and on the way, of course, I was struggling with this question of whether or not I was really going to turn my life over to God.

It started to snow. When it snows, everything gets quiet. I thought about all the life decisions I'd made since I came of age. I'd dropped out of church. I'd dropped out of high school. I had hitch-hiked around the state for a while. Of course, I had started to get high. And then there was a string of relationships that didn't work and a restless wandering from state to state. When faced with any major life decision, my process was always the same: I'd ask myself what I wanted the most, and then I went to work. When I got tired of high school, I dropped out. When I got sick of reality, I got high. When I had trouble in my personal life, I picked up and moved somewhere else. I'd gone far enough on this path that I was now in a sad state of affairs. I couldn't even hang on to a relatively easy-going woman for more than a couple of weeks.

When I looked at the record, life on my own terms didn't amount to much. Even if I surrendered everything to God, I wasn't giving up much. I felt like a guy with a car in such a bad state of repair that he was going to have to call the dump and pay them to take it away. All I had was junk, so why not let God have it?

Then a single line from the Lord's Prayer came to me, falling over my mind like the snow fell over the earth: "Thy will be done." The words drifted through me. "Thy will be done. Thy will be done."

This phrase used to make me bristle at the neck. I once thought it meant that God wouldn't have anything to do with His creatures unless they gave up their freedom and became their Creator's slaves. Why would anyone want to give up his or her free will to someone like that? Thy will be done. The words sounded different to me then. I stopped walking and let the words wash over me. Thy will be done. I'd had my fill of "freedom." All this time I'd been convinced that I was only doing what people were supposed to do—I was doing my best to get by on my own. Until that moment, I didn't believe there was any other choice for me but to keep going the way I was going, taking the edge off as best I could while I slowly drifted off the edge of sanity "one day at a time."

But now I had a choice. Thy will be done. I wasn't bound to my own will, doomed to carry it out. I could let another Power take over my life and change me. God wasn't asking me to become His slave, He was offering me a way out.

That little moment in the snow was quite powerful for me. I'd been resisting the idea of God for a long time, and now, suddenly, all that resistance was gone.

As I entered the library, I started to sob. I caught a concerned look from the librarian, so I hurried to the bathroom and locked myself in. The strength went out of my legs, and I fell to my knees. My sponsor had shown me a Third Step prayer, but I couldn't remember it. I just did the best I could:

"God, please help me. I don't want to be like this anymore."

A few days later my sponsor took me hiking and had me do my "official" Third Step. I said the prayer the way it's written in the book with him as my witness. This time, I didn't weep or have any huge insights into my life story, but I did make a formal commitment to God and to this program in front of another human being. A week earlier I had been a confirmed atheist.

As the Steps progressed, my faith and commitment to God only grew deeper. In Step Four, I had to rely on God for insight into my moral failings. In Step Five, I confessed to God everything I'd been shown. In Step Six, I spent an hour alone, meditating and asking God to show me anything I was still holding back. In Step Seven, I said another prayer and asked God to take all of me, good and bad. In Step Eight, I asked God to show me all the people I had harmed, and I wrote down their names. In Step Nine, I prayed my little butt off every time I had to face one of those people. I did not have the power or the courage to face those folks, and I didn't have the insight to say anything to them that might actually help. So I had to rely on God completely in those moments when I made amends.

Steps Ten, Eleven, and Twelve are Steps that I continue to work on daily. The longer I'm in this program, the more I feel connected to the deeper meaning of these Steps. In Step Ten, I work over the same tools I was taught in the first Nine Steps. I make a lot of amends—to my wife and son almost daily—and it never gets easier. I always have to ask for help when I've done wrong and have to go back to make right. In Step Eleven, I go to God at least twice daily and Surrender. I ask that God take my will and my life, and I ask that my heart be moved in any way God desires. When a day goes by without prayer, I end up in a foul mood, so I try to stay regular.

In Step Twelve, I do what I can to look out for the needs of others. I learn more about God and the Life of the Spirit in doing this work than

I do anywhere else in the Steps. When I get to see someone surrender him- or herself to God and find transformation in life, I feel connected to a power and purpose that far transcends anything I could ever accomplish on my own. The Spirit was around long before I arrived in this world, and it will be changing lives long after I'm gone. In the meantime, I just feel grateful that I'm able to take part in its work with the little time that I have.

God takes care of me, and I do what I can to take care of God's children.

I have not had a drink or a drug since late November 1999. I have not felt the kind of despair and pain that are natural to a life based on self-will since April 6th, 2001. I'm far from perfect. I do something stupid and selfish every day. My self-interest hasn't gone away either. So, every day, I walk with God and ask Him to carry me deeper into the Spirit of this program so that I might offer others a way out of their suffering. As time passes, I get a little better at getting out of the way and letting God do the work.

When the Twelve Steps work, they work because the person working them is willing to grow closer to God in the process. The Steps don't do anything in and of themselves; they just make certain experiences of God available to those who are willing to give God a try. For people who aren't willing to give God a try, they aren't much help; at least they weren't for me when I was flailing around in the program, just trying to scrape by on my own power.

I was the kind of guy who needs God so bad he reeks with it. But a guy like that is also a guy who won't ever admit that he needs God; he'd rather die in a mud-hole somewhere than be caught on his knees, praying. For guys like me, the church thing just won't work, not right away. We need to find God in a place where there aren't any rules. We need to feel that we have complete freedom of choice when it comes to God, otherwise we're not interested. Give us a pre-packaged God and we don't want anything to do with Him, but give us God as we understand Him and suddenly a spiritual life becomes possible for us. We can give up on ourselves and give this way of life a try. Yes, it is rather arrogant of us to resist all the wisdom of the world's religions and insist on our own experience as the "right" way, but God doesn't seem to mind.

As far as I can tell, God is happy to make peace with anyone as soon as they get tired of trying to run their own show.

The idea is not that God can be whatever anyone wants God to be. In fact, it's quite the reverse. God is who and what God is—a Power beyond human understanding. Our individual ideas about God are just works in progress. We each open our hearts and lives to God on an ongoing basis and let God teach us about Himself through our experience with Him. In living this program, we discover the Spirit at work in our daily affairs. As our relationship with God grows and changes, so does our personal theology. Because God is always speaking to us, and because there is always more to be revealed, we don't cling too tightly to any one particular idea about who God is.

The Power that changes our lives and continues to act through us to heal others cannot be fixed in place with a single rigid conception. This Power is a living Power—it cannot be defined, but it can be experienced. So we don't spend too much time trying to figure God out. We prefer to stay close to the work of the Spirit so that we can hear whatever it is that God wants to tell us next.

In the meetings I go to today, there is a rich diversity of ideas about God. We have members of a variety of faith communities and some people who are developing their own brand of spirituality, personal to them. We don't make any fuss over these matters. People are free to work out their faith in the context of their own relationship with their creator. When we get together, we don't bicker over ideas—we share experiences. Each member shares what God is doing in his or her life from a personal perspective. In this way, we all benefit from the fruits of one another's spiritual lives, regardless of our individual differences.

I know that there are many devout people who would object to our type of gathering. They would call it unorthodox, or worse. And it's true that we're rough around the edges and perhaps a bit overly permissive. We even let those grumpy, six-month dry atheists hang out with us and pester us with their questions. Actually, we like those guys. Those guys are just like me. Sooner or later, they'll hit the right kind of pain, and they'll be ready to make their surrender. I want to be there for them when that happens. It's my job.

In my own faith tradition, we think pretty highly of a guy who walked the earth a few thousand years ago. In the stories we tell about Him, He upsets the more religious members of his time by hanging out with all the lowlifes. At any given meal, our guy could be found sitting with prostitutes, tax collectors (less reputable than the IRS of today), lepers, and all sorts of unwanted types.

"Why does your master eat with all those sinners?" people asked. "If He's so spiritual, why is He hanging out with all the freaks?"

The answer He gave then is essentially the same answer we give today. God hangs out with the broken, with those in need. If you really want to meet God and see His Spirit at work, you hang out with those people, too. You do what you can for them, and when they ask, you show them how to get to know their Maker.

And, if you're smart, you don't give them any hoops to jump through. Personally, I encourage people not to worry too much about who's on the other side of the door. Just knock. He'll let you in.

GOD IS NOT WHAT YOU THINK

JAMES RYAN

The *via negativa* is the "negative way" of getting to know God. It is the way of letting go.

The basic assumption of this method is that God is much greater than anything we can imagine. As human beings of limited intelligence, we have a tendency to get attached to ideas of God that are far inferior to the reality of God.

Once we have an idea that works for us, we get lazy. We hang onto our idea, fix it in place, and start taking God for granted. We assume that our idea is good enough for practical purposes and don't bother to look any deeper into the truth.

Fixed ideas of God are like tranquilizers to the spiritual life—they slow everything down to a crawl and inhibit normal functioning. As soon as we think we know what something is, we stop paying attention to it. It is the same in our relationship with God.

Via negativa suggests that we be proactive in our search to know God and dump our intellectual baggage as soon as possible. Surrender to God all your ideas about God. Once the mind is clear, we can experience God directly with no more big ideas getting in the way.

In *via negativa*, also called the apophatic tradition, people create lists of "definitions" of God that are simply things that God is not. Authors often place ideas that the members of their faith tradition hold dear on these lists. The idea is to shake things up by poking at the ideas that are the most fixed in our minds.

What follows is an attempt to phrase an apophatic definition of God for Big Book folk. It's short and stands to be expanded, but it probably contains enough to get you started on the negative way.

Take a deep breath. Get centered. Read out loud, if only in a whisper. Read s-l-o-w-l-y, and if you find yourself wanting to defend a fixed idea, give it up.

VIA NEGATIVA **FOR BIG BOOK FOLK**

God is not a Higher Power. God is not a psychic change. God is not love, superhuman strength, or direction. God is not the Great Reality deep down within us. God is not Creative Intelligence, Universal Mind, or Spirit of Nature. God is not Creator, nor is God Maker. God is not Director, nor Principal, nor Father.

God is not a power that pulls chronic alcoholics back from the gates of death.

God is not everything, nor is God nothing. God is not God as we understand Him.

God is not freedom from mental obsession. God is not a spiritual experience.

God is not a miracle of healing. God is not the Presence of Infinite Power and Love.

God is not a Fellowship of the Spirit. God is not the Road of Happy Destiny.

God is not a defense against the first drink.

ADD MORE *VIA NEGATIVA* DEFINITIONS BELOW:

At that, Jesus led His disciples to the place called Gethsemane.

Jesus: I am going over there to pray. You sit here *while I'm at prayer.*

Then He took Peter and the two sons of Zebedee with Him, and He grew sorrowful and deeply distressed.

Jesus: My soul is overwhelmed with grief, to the point of death. Stay here and keep watch with Me.

He walked a little farther and finally fell prostrate and prayed.

Jesus: Father, *this is the last thing I want.* If there is any way, please take this bitter cup from Me. Not My will, but Yours be done.

When He came back to the disciples, He saw that they were asleep. *Peter awoke a little less confident and slightly chagrined.*

Jesus (to Peter): So you couldn't keep watch with Me for just one short hour? *Now maybe you're learning:* the spirit is willing, but the body is weak. Watch and pray and take care that you are not pulled down during a time of testing.

With that, Jesus returned to *His secluded spot* to pray again.

Jesus: Father, if there is no other way for this cup to pass without My drinking it—*then not My will,* but Yours be done.

— *Matthew 26:36-42*

SURRENDER
JOEL MCKERROW

There comes a moment in every life
when there is nowhere left to turn. When that which once
appeared so full and overflowing has been tap rust run dry.
A hole in the pipes so many years ago, never fixed, leaking water;
it was only a matter of time.
And still we sit holding cupped hands out to the drip of a tap that has
chosen no longer to flow.
How hard it is to leave what was. We would place our mouth around the pipe,
suck rust if we
could. I have seen men lose themselves for less.
Rusty insides, every one of us.
Empty belly,
desperate look in the eye.
Dry taps and we are not letting go.
Letting go—
if there were a manual it would be well read.
Well read and used less. Used less. Useless.
Letting go,
        they are two nervous words.
Only ever said with slight tremor, sheen of sweat, shake of hand.
Letting go is most often akin not to the release of one's hand from the tap,
but the need to cut the whole limb rigor-mortis and clinging to the rust.
Do not tell me this is easy.
Letting go is never easy. Never has been.
It is the cut of flesh.
Surrender feels more like a curse than a promise.
A knife stuck in deep.
Turn your head away,
find a new source of water and life.
The tap wishes it were a river.
Find a river.
Lap at its edge,
stick your hand stump in its waters,
you will soon forget the tap and its empty promise.
Surrender is a bitter pill,
        but I know this, it does not taste like rust.
Freedom always tastes bitter to begin with.
Bitter and better than anything in this world.

SABOTAGE, SURRENDER, HEALING

AARON EDWARDS

"Blessed are the poor in spirit..." Learning the meaning behind this first beatitude from Jesus's Sermon on the Mount is essential for us to be able to learn how to live a dying life instead of a living death. We have the opportunity (if we're ready) to explore all the ways in which we sabotage ourselves in our fleshly pursuits, which forces us to face the choice between breakdown and breakthrough. *The Message* translates this beatitude like this: "You're blessed when you're at the end of your rope. With less of you there is more of God and His rule." (Matthew 5:3)

Spiritual poverty recognizes that all we have and all we are is a total gift from God. We are totally dependent on a good and loving God who is in charge of the universe and in charge of our lives. Are we ready to acknowledge a total dependence on God? Are we ready to admit that we don't have all the answers in our own right? Not until we get to the end of our rope, which usually means sabotaging ourselves, which leads to surrender, which leads to healing.

From our experience, we are always in one of these three stages. Each stage feels very different than the others, but each is necessary, and each holds hope.

Sabotage—This usually happens when we start believing we have it all figured out. We start to get a taste of worldly success, we start to count our gains as gains, and we start to distance ourselves from that sweet place of surrendering to our dependence on God that we once believed would last forever. Fear begins to set in. Fear that God doesn't exist or that His cost will be too high for us to make the journey. Fear of anything, really, seems heavy and exhausting. We become weighed down with anxiety and pressure (both of which are not even real things, they are simply the pain of resisting what is). That's when we fall off our chosen path and begin to live lives of quiet desperation, wondering what happened to leave us in such a malaise, which is essentially a living death. This is the process of sabotaging ourselves until we have no choice but to get back to the place of...

Surrender—Now we are at the end of our rope again. It once again becomes crystal clear that we cannot experience the peace and joy that our souls long for unless we realize that we are not the ones in charge of our lives. We have to let go of everything we thought would satisfy us externally. We tried to manage our lives and discipline ourselves, but it didn't do for us what we thought it would do. So now we have to become poor in spirit. We have to die emotionally and spiritually, be crucified with Christ. This can make us feel like we are going to lose everything. We have to jump off the cliff, so to speak, in hopes that God will catch us. And He does, and everything makes sense again. God welcomes this spirit of surrender and lets us know that He has always had us in the palm of His hand. We can now experience His nurturing Spirit, and so begins the...

Healing—This is the place where we get to see the point and purpose of sabotage and surrender. It all makes sense. We see that God has never left us. He uses all three stages to point us back to Himself. He works all things together for good. We stop walking around in a living death (a mere existence for the purpose of continued pain relief) and start to live a dying life (a bold existence for the purpose of accomplishing what you were made to accomplish, with the help of a Higher Power whose yoke is light). But because of our tricky natures and sheer forgetfulness, the beauty of His purpose for our lives begins to fade. This stage of healing eventually stops being an experience and turns into a memory. We can only live off of our last surrender for so long until we once again start to sabotage ourselves. And so the cycle continues.

A WAY TO COME ALIVE

ANDY GULLAHORN

I was always confused by the idea of losing your life to gain it. At least, I was confused by it until I really felt like I lost it. I lost my pride, my self-image, my good name, my "righteousness," my history of being the good kid, and my right to be respected. The weird thing was that when it happened, it felt like I didn't actually lose anything. That isn't totally true. I felt like the only things I lost were things that were worth losing—like losing excess weight or baggage that left me feeling liberated and healthier. And the life that came out of that surrender was easily brighter and better than the one I started with.

How many times will I have to experience that phenomenon to fully trust that good will happen each time I live in the posture of surrender?

WHY YOU BROUGHT ME HERE
A SONG

ANDY GULLAHORN & JASON GRAY

I know I'll get an answer that I won't understand
If I ask that your intentions be made clear
I know your plans are greater and in that greater plan
Lie the reasons why you brought me here

This story would be different if it were only mine to write
There are secrets I would never volunteer
But the secrets lose their power when they have no place to hide
Maybe that is why you brought me here

Ohhh I hope you know what you're doing
You brought me here

It's a mess of my own making, I fully realize
And the consequences shake my heart with fear
But if I was happy with the way things were then I'd put up a fight
I guess I'm grateful that you brought me here

Ohhh, all I see are the ruins
But as the smoke starts to clear
I hope you know what you're doing
You brought me here

It's hard to raise the white flag but it's harder to believe
That surrendering is worth the sacrifice
Because the very thing I always feared would be the death of me
Was a way to come alive

It hurts to be so broken but it's bearable somehow
As the grounds to prove I'm worthy disappear
I always heard You loved me, I think I know it now
It's a reason why You brought me here
Love's a reason why You brought me here

DOWNLOAD LINK: HTTP://BIT.LY/1VLM6PH

"Lay yourself *bare, facedown to the ground*, in humility before the Lord; and He will lift your head *so you can stand tall.*"

—James 4:10

"The moment I try to work out a formula for surrender, it moves so I have to spiritually stay open to it."

—Matthew Russell

SURRENDER
PIETER VAN WAARDE

O Lord,
Not sure what's coming next.

Not sure who
      (or what)
            I can count on.

I have made my share of promises
      that lie broken and irredeemable,
           feeding my guilt and shame.

It pains me to know what I've become
      to myself and to those whose love I spurned
           …dare I even mention you?

I have no business asking,
      and you have every right to ignore—
           I deserve the mess I have created.

Yet I cling to a lingering hope
      of mercy offered
           to those who deserve it least.

I believe I might qualify.

Therefore,
      I surrender
           to it and to you…
               hold me fast.
                  It is all I have left.

WHAT I REALLY WANT IS A LIFE WITHOUT FAITH

GREGG TAYLOR

To be honest, I really don't want to live by faith. I think what I really want is to live a life without faith.

When I look at what scares me, so much of it has do with a violation of my deep need to be in control and to predict a future that's in my own best interest. So to be honest, faith is a real problem for me. Why? Because faith can only begin at the point when I'm willing to give up my need to control what I cannot control, and when I become willing to surrender my need to have a predictable future. At its core, faith is about trusting something or someone BECAUSE I am not in control and BECAUSE I cannot predict the future.

I think I need to listen to my fear so I can learn what it means to have faith.

Fear, what do you have to teach me? You are teaching me that one of the things I need in order to overcome my fear is faith. But when the thing I need to overcome my fear is something I'd rather not have, it's a problem for me. Something's gotta give.

Fear, what do you have to teach me? You are teaching me that my soul yearns to trust a God I cannot see, cannot control, and cannot predict. You are helping me learn how wide and how deep and how rich is a relationship with a God who invites me into mystery and who always sustains me with His love, which in my mind is mysterious enough.

So, God who I cannot control, God who I cannot predict, and God who I cannot see but who I know is with me and within me, here's my prayer today: Grant me the serenity to accept the things I cannot change, the courage to change the things I can, and please give me the wisdom to know the difference.

I SURRENDER

AARON EDWARDS

For ten years, I suffered from an absolutely debilitating condition called Trigeminal Neuralgia (TN). The trigeminal nerve branches across the side of the face and is responsible for both sensory and motor functions. TN is known as the "suicide disease"; it is a neuropathic disorder characterized by episodes of intense pain—I am talking painful pain. Neuroscientists describe this condition as one of the most painful known to man because the brain reacts as if there is an exposed nerve being triggered over and over again, creating an electric-shock effect in the cheek, lips, and gums. Needless to say, this made everyday life and even the most menial tasks feel impossible.

As a husband, father, and pastor, I would constantly try to compensate for the screaming pain going on inside my face. I would pretend that I could manage my pain and would basically put all my effort into just keeping it together. For the first six years of my condition, my primary mission was to eliminate my pain in any way possible. After seeing countless specialists and naturalists with little to no relief, I opted to see a pain management doctor. She prescribed hydrocodone, which did not make the electric-shock sensation go away, but it did take the edge off the pain.

It did not take long for me to develop a dependence on the medication, and I remained on some form of opiates for the next two years. One day I woke up and my neuralgia wasn't as active as it usually was, so I decided not to take the medication that day. By midday, I felt like I had the flu; I was sore all over and had chills. It hit me that I was going through withdrawal. Many people in our community are in recovery—though others are still in the throes of their addiction—and friends have tried to explain to me what it feels like to detox from heroin or other opiate-based drugs. That day in 2007, I began to understand exactly what they had been talking about. I was supposed to be the pastor that ministered to the addicted; instead, I entered into solidarity with the addicts.

The idea of withdrawal terrified me, so I decided to do what made most sense—I took a couple of pills. Thirty minutes later I felt fine. This created a discovery that scared me even more—I was full on addicted to opiates.

My addiction was easy to justify because, after all, I had the worst pain known to man (there's a reason it's called the suicide disease), and because I had taken my medication as prescribed. But my withdrawal symptoms haunted me everyday. I couldn't stop thinking about it, and I made sure not to skip a day because I did not want to feel that way again. I also made sure to have the refill prescription on hand before I ran out because now, on top of being consumed with the pain, I was also consumed with the pain medication.

This was my process for the next few months, constantly running from the pain while simultaneously running from withdrawal. One Sunday at church, I decided to out myself. I told my community that I was in a dilemma. I said that I needed the medication for pain, but I also needed it to avoid getting "dope-sick." It is amazing how much room the Spirit has to dance around when we go beneath the facades and get real. I was fully embraced by my brothers and sisters and walked away feeling thankful and filled with grace.

The day after that beautiful church service, I woke up overwhelmed with the notion that it was time to stop all medication completely. There was no doubt in my mind that this was a nudge from the Holy Spirit. The first thing I asked God was, "Can we wait and have this conversation after you heal me from my condition?" But there was no escaping the fact that it was time. His Spirit spoke and my spirit accepted. However, my mind was being dragged kicking and screaming. This was going to suck so bad! I had butterflies in my stomach, knowing how bad it had felt a few months before after just half a day without the meds. At the same time, my spirit was whispering to my mind that there was going to be a gift in this for me.

The next day a friend told me I could use her little fishing cabin in Galveston to detox. I called a very close friend of mine, Matt, and asked if he would go with me in case I got too sick to take care of myself. He immediately accepted the invitation. Things were working out quite effortlessly, and a couple of days later we were off.

The day we left for Galveston was the first morning in over two years (besides the aforementioned day) that I didn't take the pain meds as soon as I woke up. It was also the morning I awoke to piercing pain and waves of fire rolling through my face. Of course. It's a strange phenomenon; when freedom is in sight, slavery tends to bear down hard, wanting to keep us enslaved. As miserable as captivity is, we find ways to get comfortable in its familiarity, making the idea of "letting go" and birthing into freedom terrifying. If freedom weren't so free, if we could control it just a bit, that would make it an easier choice.

The reality was quickly setting in. My stomach tangled up, reminding me of what it felt like to be sent to the principal's office as a fifth grader: pure dread. I remember kissing my wife and kids goodbye while thinking, "There is NO WAY this isn't going to be really bad!"

By the time we got there, I was already feeling horrible. Even the hair on my arms felt sore to the touch. I broke into a cold sweat, and to be honest, I couldn't tell you if it was from withdrawal or simply from the fear of it. I paced back and forth, wearing out the floor of the cabin. My body was at a fevered pitch of surging electricity and my mind was racing to stay ahead of it, angling for a distraction. I turned on the television and, ten seconds later, turned it off. I couldn't sit still. I remembered that I brought my Bible—surely the Psalms would be comforting in a time like this. I was able to read for about thirty seconds, which, to the Bible's credit, was three times longer than the TV lasted. I was being called into my pain, but I didn't feel I was called into it alone. I had a good sense God was sitting with me through this one.

I resumed pacing. Honestly, I couldn't have imagined any of the pain I was going through unless I had gone through it. Not that I am recommending the experience, because at this point I was thinking about running my head through a wall. I took up my new pacing habit outside on the deck. The air was windy and salty. I kept walking. Then something happened. The first beatitude in the Sermon on the Mount says, "You're blessed when you're at the end of your rope. With less of you, there is more of God and His rule" (Matthew 5:3, *The Message*). I have heard people say, "When you are at the end of your rope, tie a knot and swing," but I wasn't enjoying this ride. I had a choice to make. It was at the end of myself where my ego succumbed to my spirit, and my spirit succumbed to His Spirit. I let go. I surrendered.

I sat in a chair on the deck with my arms down, palms up. Words will never be adequate to describe what happened next. God revealed himself, and God was Love, and Love washed over me, so soothingly, wave after wave. My chest opened up to All That Is, and I received. It was like taking everything I ever hoped and dreamed God was and multiplying it times a million. Not only did He fill me with love and peace and hope, He was genuinely glad that I was open to receive it! Overwhelmed is an understatement. I was both bawling and laughing, both within myself and without. And in that place and time, I was free from withdrawal and even from the pain of my neuralgia. I felt like I had been taken into what Paul refers to as the third heaven. In that moment, I became clearly aware that everything I'd ever experienced had been a part of a perfect path and that nothing was wrong. He has always been making all things new. He is on a rescue mission that we cannot thwart.

I looked out at the sun's reflection on the water and saw millions of shimmering diamonds in the wakes on the bay. I remember literally putting my hand to my chest with my mouth agape because of the sheer awe I felt at the gift of seeing the sun reflecting off the water. My friend Matt was standing in the corner of the deck, graciously giving me my space, and maybe somewhat concerned about my tears and blubbering smile. I looked at him and said, "You're not going to believe what is happening between me and God right now." I started to tell him about the mystical experience I was having, and as I was telling him I started to feel the withdrawals creeping back into my skin. I started laughing. I said, "I think I had to step out of the Spirit in order to tell you about being in the Spirit." For the next two days, I bounced back and forth between discomfort and sheer bliss. We went to Wal-Mart for a few supplies and it took all the willpower I had not to walk up to total strangers, put my hands on their cheeks, and ask them if they knew how loved they were.

I listened to a lot of music at the cabin for the next couple of days with fresh ears and new vision. I read a lot of Scripture, and amazingly, after being rerouted from using the Bible as an escape, I couldn't get enough of it. I read about being crucified with Christ and knew that it is much more than an idea or doctrine. It is an experience of dying to self and being risen to be in Christ. Jesus showed us in a beautiful, grandiose way what we are invited to do spiritually everyday.

My body spent the next few weeks working the rest of the toxins out of my body, while also relearning how to live with TN. But my relationship to my pain changed completely. Instead of running from it, I learned to lean into it, to be present with it, to allow it to be a passageway to the place where His strength becomes perfected in my weakness. My life has never been the same. I am so thankful to know that God is Love.

That was October of 2007. For the next several years, I went through pain and growth. In 2011, because of God's grace, I was given the opportunity to undergo a surgical procedure called microvascular decompression. The surgery was successful and I no longer have trigeminal neuralgia. My life is changed. I know how blessed I am. I know that there are countless other people who have chronic pain that may never end on this side of the Kingdom. But I also know that our pain doesn't happen to us, it happens for us.

I am thankful to have lived with the pain and am thankful to now live without it.

I am thankful for the pain medicine and happy to live without it.

I am thankful for my path, for the times I am far and the times I am near.

I am thankful that surrender births resurrection.

FORGIVE OTHERS

PIETER VAN WAARDE

It was probably four years ago when I walked out of the counselor's office with a backpack full of rocks. I was a bit depressed. I was losing sleep and overly sensitive at home, and so I did what I often encourage others to do. I went to my counselor to sort some things out. Part of what was making me depressed was that I was doing a lot of discounting. I said things like, "I feel a bit foolish about being here. I am a pastor with 25 plus years of ministry experience. I should be able to work through this on my own, but I can't seem to get ahead of it."

The counselor was trying to help me find some perspective and remind me that each of the issues I was processing was, in fact, complicated and significant, and that minimizing my experience was not helpful. I think it was my second or third session with the therapist when he told me to bring a backpack and a decent sized rock for each challenge I was dealing with at the time.

There were six to seven pretty big issues I was processing. It wasn't that any one challenge was overwhelming in and of itself. They were each significant, but bearable. It was the cumulative effect of them all weighing me down at the same time that made it feel so overwhelming. After two weeks, the counselor's point was well made. No wonder I was tired and cranky and feeling out of sorts. I was letting my issues get the best of me.

I think, for many of us, unforgiveness functions in the same way. We carry around resentment and bitterness about personal violations that have occurred in our lives:

Ways in which we were hurt (emotionally or physically).

Ways in which we were ignored or slighted.

Ways in which we were made fun of or teased.

Or, more seriously, ways in which we were abused and / or abandoned, leaving scars that remain to this day.

As a result of these hurts, we are resentful and angry against those who were cruel. The problem with this is that unforgiveness directed toward the perpetrators actually becomes a burden or weight that we, the victims, end up carrying. We think it is our way of getting even with those who hurt us, but it is actually part of the excess weight we carry around with us. We are the ones who suffer in the end. We add to our own heartache when we hold on to this stuff. It reminds me of a legend about two priests.

Before the days of bridges, part of the priestly duties was helping the elderly across streams or rivers when they needed to cross to the other side. As the legend goes, there were two priests (one older and one younger) who were walking through the countryside. They happened upon an old woman standing at the bank of a river. As was customary, the older priest offered to carry the woman for the five-minute walk to the other side. It must have felt like an eternity to the priest, though, because from the moment she got on his back she did nothing but complain.

She complained that he was going too slowly, that he wasn't carrying her high enough, that he was hurting her legs, that he was worthless and stupid and weak. The younger priest just watched in disbelief. When they reached the other shore, the older priest put the woman down, fixed his robes, and bowed before returning on his journey.

As they walked, the younger priest remarked, "I cannot believe the way she treated you!" The older priest said nothing. Another five minutes passed and the younger priest piped up again, "I mean it. If she had talked that way to me, I would have been tempted to drop her into the water. How ungrateful!" The older priest said nothing.

The younger priest kept mumbling and grumbling about the old woman for another thirty minutes. Finally, the older priest, turning to his companion, said, "My brother. I stopped carrying the woman more than half an hour ago. Why, are you still carrying her?"

Forgiveness can be really hard to give, even when it comes to the mundane challenges of everyday life, but when we can let an offense go and lay it down, something truly remarkable can take place.

When learning about forgiveness, perhaps it can be helpful to know what forgiveness is not.

- Forgiveness does not mean that you excuse what happened.

- Forgiveness does not mean that there shouldn't be any consequences.

- Forgiveness does not mean that you will forget what took place.

- Forgiveness does not mean you turn off your feelings.

- Forgiveness does not mean the relationship is automatically restored.

- Forgiveness does not mean you don't learn from the experience.

- Forgiveness does not mean everything is okay (or okay forever).

In short, forgiveness is about your journey with what happened to you and making room for God to do His part. I think Paul summarizes it well in Romans 12:18-19:

> If it is possible, as far as it depends on you, live at peace with everyone. Do not take revenge, my dear friends, but leave room for God's wrath, for it is written: "It is mine to avenge; I will repay," says the Lord. (NIV)

That last part is the crux of it—to trust God to take care of it. This seems impossible. And truth be told, forgiving others is one of the most counter-intuitive things we do in life. Maybe that is one of the reasons there is so much in scripture about it. Jesus even made it a centerpiece in His model prayer, connecting our experience of His forgiveness with our willingness to extend forgiveness to others.

> And forgive us our debts, as we also have forgiven those our debtors. (Matthew 6:12)

You may be wondering how this actually happens. How do people get to a place of forgiveness? This is a great and seemingly basic question, and it stands to reason that if this is so important, there should be a reasonably simple answer. Unfortunately, there is not. I can describe the process simply enough, but I think at some fundamental level, before we get into the particulars, we have to understand this is basically spiritual work. It is grounded in God's working in and through us. It's soul work! And like all soul work, it is both a spiritual gift and a human decision-making process. God is the inspiration, God enables, and then we choose whether or not we will cooperate with that work.

I think Peter captures the heart of it:

> Finally, all of you, be like-minded, love one another, be compassionate and humble. Do not repay evil with evil or insult with insult. On the contrary, repay evil with blessing, because to this you were called so that you may inherit a blessing. For, "Whoever would love life and see good days must keep their tongue from evil and their lips from deceitful speech. (1 Peter 3:8-10)

Notice the intertwining of God's calling and our responsiveness. If you don't buy any of that, you can try and do it with your own strength, though I'm not sure how long that will last. At some point, on some hard day, your own human weakness will get the best of you. You'll plot revenge. You'll obsess over what happened. You'll take up your backpack and start the cycle of hatred and bitterness all over again.

So, at some level, this process has to begin with a confession that we can't really do this in our own strength, and that happens by just admitting it: "God, I cannot do this without You! But with You and by Your strength, I can begin to make some progress." Depending on what you are dealing with and how well-developed your alternative coping mechanisms are, you might find yourself right here for some time. Some people call this the stage of being willing to be willing. Then there comes that point of personal decision. God can meet us, but He does not force us. There is a dynamic of human freedom where we can choose to cooperate or resist. We can choose to let it go or hang on to it. That choice is up to us. Now, I think it is important to say that this is not a once and done kind of deal. This decision is one we will have to revisit and re-decide time and again.

I read a story about a woman who was very much mistreated by her former husband. After her divorce, she went through counseling and started the process of forgiveness. She was a Christ-follower and had watched many friends walk through similar circumstances and get eaten up by bitterness. She didn't want to go that way so she sincerely engaged the process. She wasn't flippant about it. In fact, she was quite deliberate. After a number of months, she felt resolved that she had worked through the process and had done what she needed to do. It was really hard, but she felt great about where she landed. She thanked the counselor and started to move on with her life.

A couple of years down the road, however, she started having nightmares. She was confused and frustrated because she thought she had already released all the "stuff" to God. So, why was this still haunting her?

She went back to her counselor and started talking about what she was feeling and processing, and in the midst of the conversation she discovered another layer. Although she had truly forgiven him for what he had done to her, she discovered that she was still harboring some secret hopes for retribution and revenge. She still wanted him to feel some of the same measure of pain and fear and anguish that he had inflicted on her. She even found some of those thoughts creeping their way into her prayers: "O God, let him hurt like he hurt me!"

So here she was again, having to release everything to God, not because her ex deserved it, but rather so that the anger she was feeling wouldn't come back and spoil her own spirit. So again she found herself saying, "I release him to You, O God. This is Yours. I trust You with him. I forgive him.

I can almost feel the tension we all feel about this. Because, on an emotional level, it feels like we are letting people get away with things that they shouldn't be able to get away with. I understand, I really do. I have carried around my own rocks. This isn't theoretical to me; this is my life, too.

So let me say it again. Releasing something or someone to God is not another way of tossing the problem aside, rather it is entrusting the situation to the One who never sleeps, the One who sees into the souls of people, the One who can bring conviction and repentance, and the One who holds all our eternal destinies in His hands. And when you think about it in that way, it is actually the most powerful thing we can do with anything and everything we are holding on to. And not only do we get to put down our backpacks of stones, we spare our hearts from turning to stone as well.

"O Eternal One, I know our lives are in Your hands. It is not in us to direct our own steps—*we need You.*"

—*Jeremiah 10:23*

WORDS OF COMFORT AND PEACE

Blessed are the spiritually poor—the kingdom of heaven is theirs.
Blessed are those who mourn—they will be comforted.
Blessed are the meek and gentle—they will inherit the earth.
Blessed are those who hunger and thirst for righteousness—they
    will be filled.
Blessed are the merciful—they will be shown mercy.
Blessed are those who are pure in heart—they will see God.
Blessed are the peacemakers—they will be called children of God.
Blessed are those who are persecuted because of righteousness—
    the kingdom of heaven is theirs.

——*Matthew 5:3-10*, The Voice

***

You are sent into the world under a crown of blessing.
With one hand I hold you up,
with the other I cover you.
You are safe with Me,
Whatever you surrender falls into My hands.
Let go. I have you.
I bless you, I bless your life.

——*Kelly Hall*

Waking Up

CURRICULUM

KIM ENGELMANN

"Be like house servants waiting for their master to come back from his honeymoon, awake and ready to open the door when he arrives and knocks. Lucky the servants whom the master finds on watch! He'll put on an apron, sit them at the table, and serve them a meal, sharing his wedding feast with them. It doesn't matter what time of the night he arrives; they're awake—and so blessed!"

—Luke 12:35-38, The Message

THEOLOGICAL IMPLICATIONS

The film talks about shaking ourselves to open our eyes and see what we are really experiencing in life. Life can be routine and boring, or it can be filled with experiences of immense poignancy and awe. Seeing life as a miracle, seeing another person for who they truly are and allowing wonder and beauty to overwhelm us, takes divine intervention. Like Saul who had scales fall from his eyes and lived life in a completely different way afterward, we need that touch of divine grace to wake us up to Jesus in our midst. This Scripture is very telling. When we are awake we are able to 1) let Jesus in, 2) allow Jesus to serve us by receiving His bounty, 3) be blessed by celebrating with wonder the joy of being in close fellowship with Him. It's easier to stay awake if we know we might actually encounter Jesus at any minute. It's easier to stay awake if we are looking forward to a party with Him! When I am in relationship with another and I am awake, I see Jesus in that individual. When I am asleep, all I notice is one more person.

QUESTIONS FOR REFLECTION

Do you have a way of telling if, on any given day, you are awake or asleep? What signs indicate that you are asleep? That you are awake?

There are many reasons for living life with our eyes closed. Stress is a big factor, along with discouragement and pain of many kinds. With this knowledge, how might we learn to wake up when we sense that we are numbing ourselves to life?

Think about a time you remember being fully awake to life. What awed you? What gave you joy? Who was there, and how did you see them?

Receiving what has already been given is hard for those of us who haven't let go of our own need to pursue, strive, and fix. How does staying awake keep us on our toes in terms of being able to receive more fully the gift of life that is already ours?

PRAYER

Jesus, You were awake all the time. You knew exactly what God was telling You to do and You never took anyone for granted. You were fully alive and totally aware. Let the scales of numbness fall from my eyes that I might take in the gift of life fully and live every day with my spiritual eyes wide open. Amen

WRITE YOUR OWN PRAYER HERE

A BLESSING FOR WAKING UP

KELLY HALL

At times I ask, *sometimes repeatedly,*
for You to come alive in me.
I imagine You would crack the whip, sound the charge,
or blow a gust of wind to lurch me in the right direction . . .
and You might. I am not sure.

There are days I am no more than a body in endless waters—
suspended,
        soaked lungs,
        dangling limbs—
I might even believe that I wasn't dead afloat, but actually swimming
        at the time You pulled me out of the deep
            (or maybe I was in the shallow end).

Fill me with Your breath, resuscitate me,
remind me that I am with You, and You are with me.

Let me be with You as You are with me:
        closer than my beliefs and ideas, my thoughts
        and expectations—
            Let me reside in You,
            and become more constant in my faith—
                I am Yours
                Eternal in love, let us remain
                    awake, together.

"We may ignore, but we can nowhere evade, the presence of God. The world is crowded with Him. He walks everywhere *incognito*. And the *incognito* is not always easy to penetrate. The real labor is to remember to attend. In fact to come awake. Still more to remain awake."

—*C. S. Lewis*

WAKING UP
JOEL MCKERROW

It takes me forever to get out of bed.
Like, forever.
I am no morning person,
no 6 a.m. run and yoga,
no focused time of existence
before the work day begins.
Oh I have tried,
given myself alarm clocks
and new year's resolutions
which I do keep,
for a day,
a week,
occasionally two.
The soft call of sheets and cuddling wife
and warm feet and fluffy pillows, it is too much for my willpower.
I have lost before I start,
before I can even reach to turn off the alarm.
Or perhaps I have won, I tell myself as my eyelids close again.
And just so you know,
my wife is worse than I.
And just so you know,
we are expecting
in April.
Now that shall be a wake-up call.
My guess is that screaming babies
shall have more power over me
than the soft dulcet wake-up tones of my iPhone.
I have had to awaken over and over in my life
and not just from bedtime sleeps.
Ignorance is a slumber too
and so is entitlement,
so is the rightness of me, the wrongness of everyone else who disagrees,
so is the western dream.
Over and over I have felt the harsh light of daytime reality peep through
                the curtains,
call me to wake up, untwist myself from comfortable sheets and
                affluent pillows.
These mornings are twice as hard,

when all I want to do is roll over,
pretend the world outside my window does not exist.
My eyelids close again.
Those times it also took a crying baby to move me,
a crying baby in Burma,
a homeless man in Sydney,
a prostitute in Port Kembla,
a refugee from West Papua,
a gay man turned straight, a straight man turned gay,
an addict who loved another addict,
These were the alarm clocks I could not just turn off.
They kept at me again and again, until I awoke, slowly, over many years.

ROUSE ME FROM MY SLEEP

PHUC LUU

The alarm goes off, and many of us hit the snooze button. Whoever invented this option gave us a ridiculous choice. We set our alarms in order to wake up, and whenever we hit the snooze, we are basically saying to ourselves we don't want to do what we wanted to do in the first place. Why not just set the alarm for five minutes later and wake up then instead of disturbing our sleep? This is the contradiction of the snooze button! But my point is not to criticize its use, but to look at how figuratively "pushing snooze" delays our experiences of "waking up" in life.

Just imagine this picture with me: We have two selves. Not a split personality. Not some kind of dual nature. But we are both who we are now and who we need to be. We often imagine ourselves like this. "One day I will do such and such," or, "One day I will be there," or, "One day I will be with that person." We talk about our future selves as another person, but that person is simply us growing and maturing into the persons we want to be, or even better, need to be. We are growing into ourselves, like butterflies from caterpillars. This is our process of development and growth. The person we are now is hopefully different than the person we were at the age of four.

This process happens in stages and is accompanied by a series of "waking up" moments. Our bodies change when we are teenagers and we "wake up" to the possibilities provided by sexuality, dating, love, and so on. We graduate from college or get a demanding job and we "wake up" to the realities of paying bills, being responsible with our money, and balancing all the demands of life. Those of us who are married come to realize the responsibilities of loving another person, sharing life, and raising children. Each stage is a rousing of the soul, and we are changed by it. Life is a series of "getting up."

However, sometimes we can get stuck at one transition in life and it seems as though we cannot move on. When there is some kind of traumatic or difficult life event, we often find ourselves held back. It is as if the alarm did not go off and we remain asleep, avoiding the difficulties of the world. Sometimes we think it was a better world before we experienced these difficulties, and moving backward seems like a better option than moving forward. So we hit the snooze button and go back to bed.

Then a mismatch happens between who we are and who we should be. Some of us are childish adults. We shun responsibility. We respond to life with temper tantrums. We cannot deal with our emotions. We become impatient and want immediate satisfaction (and sometimes even immediate satisfaction is not fast enough). We want our mommies or daddies. Life tries to wake us up by giving us challenges and realities we must and ought to face. It presents a crisis which may actually be an opportunity to grow that is viewed as an annoyance. It's a buzzing alarm. Time to wake up! But we hit the snooze, go back to sleep.

However, the consequences for this habit are dire. When we get into this practice of not waking when we should, we are telling ourselves that we cannot move on to the next stage in life. We find ourselves making the same mistakes over and over again, and often wonder why we end up in the same situation. There is a cycle of repeated poor choices, repeated bad relationships, and repeated disappointments. Why is it that we cannot comprehend the situation in which we find ourselves? Our friends try to rouse us. Our family members try to wake us. But we still slumber. Life throws things our way. But then we sometimes interpret the situation as unfair or harsh or bad luck, whatever keeps us from really hearing what is being said. We don't yet "get it."

"If you have ears, then listen!" Many people heard these words from the Master, but these words were mere sounds that washed over them. The few who took it to heart were called disciples. These were the men and women who retreated privately to hear the Master talk about another reality, a world for which they would need to "wake up" in order to experience fully. There was another way to live and to be. This is why Jesus often said to His disciples, "The Kingdom of God is within you." It is a reality into which we are growing—that is, if we are willing to listen, to really listen.

There have been moments in my life that I have misinterpreted and events that I have blamed others for, and in moments of reflection I realized I was not being the person I want to be. There are but three options: retreat (i.e. hitting the snooze button), change the world, or wake up. Trying to change the world is equivalent to just saying alarm clocks don't exist and that we can wake up any time we please. It is saying that whatever realities are out there must be bad. I must do what I can to correct the system. However, often it is not the system that is broken, but you and me Broken people need to be cared for, not fixed. Jesus was a physician of the soul, not a political leader in the ways of Stalin or Mao Tse-tung. He did not need to overthrow one party to make room for another. His mission was to bring another system into reality. This system was healing the person: "Behold, I am making all things new."

This is why the third option is the best. People who are successful—I mean success as more than wealth—do not let life act upon them, but rather they shape their character in order to respond to life the way they should. They are honest with themselves about their limitations and about their need to move into a new stage in their lives. For them, life is a series of awakenings; it is a series of realizations and opened possibilities. But this can only be done through many other realizations:

> the realization that we are not alone.
> the realization that we are meant to be more than who we presently are.
> the realization that God loves us and wants the best for us.

It is on these very basic and very important blocks that our entire character is built.

Take some time today to note the important events in your life. Are these wake-up calls? Are these opportunities—either opportunities missed or yet to be taken? What is it that you need to hear? Whose counsel do you need to take? What shape should your prayers take? Are they prayers of crisis or prayers of opportunity? What can be learned about God, the world, and ourselves?

Our lives are a series of movements from one scene to another, and each transition is assisted by an awakening. Characters who cannot overcome challenges are considered tragic, but those who conquer are labeled heroic. We all move in Shakespearian ways from one character to the other, playing many parts in life. But we are not left to our own devices. We are assisted by a Director who also appears to us as one of the characters. In this way, we are always reminded to awaken, sometimes by a gentle nudge and sometimes by a strong prod, but in every moment, we are always loved.

A PRAYER FOR THE RISING
PHUC LUU

God of the dawn and new day
Help me to rise from my slumbers
So I may find rest in You
Move my heart toward Your eternal comfort
With each moment, engaging my soul
Help my blurred vision to see
And my cloudy head to understand
Arise the sleeper in me,
Awaken me from my tomb
Amen

"Waking up is becoming unbound, and unbinding those places that keep us separate from love and each other."

—*Matt Russell*

"Waking up is what happened when I sought intimacy with God."

—*John Doss*

A MOMENT

SHELLEE COLEY

There is a single moment when you realize that every moment in life goes exactly as it must in order for you to properly feel each consecutive moment.

And when that realization sets in, you can then consider all things as opportunities to learn and grow and expand. You blink a little slower so that you can take in every color that speeds by you in a flurry and tuck it away behind your eyelids for later. You breathe a little deeper so that you can feel the caverns of your lungs waiting for you to send another shot of life into them. And most of all you begin to walk more purposefully, stopping to engage only with those hearts and souls that breathe into you new life with even their very presence.

This is the moment when nothing else matters except love and intention, and you let go of all that no longer serves your highest good, and bring into your sphere the expansion of life where you have plenty of room to grow and change into the soul lover you were brought here to be.

And when you become aware of and begin to cross paths with those souls that you were brought here to love, a new moment arises in you, and the realization of depth sets in. *No longer do you desire to control other beings, forcing them to love you, because the desire for the deepest of connections outweighs control, and the waiting becomes the gift.* Waiting for the beauty of a connection to come into its perfect timing of birth and life. Creation. And when that happens, souls can then move fluidly in and out and all around each other, creating masterpieces, as love permits, in order to give each other exactly what is needed at the perfect time.

And so in this newly created space, the simple and yet complex act of a kiss becomes a momentary connection between yourself and another, passing by and seeing something deeper within their soul, as opposed to a promise that ties you to a heart for the life of its body.

And even greater still, when the time comes for two souls to come together in passion, and the bond of bodily love is created, it is just exactly that . . .

Creating.

Art crafted by two souls to be admired only by them and to be used intentionally for what needs to be healed within each of them.

For love is art, and art is healing. But on the deepest level, life is art and should be moveable and bendable and shapeable. And although art is most certainly subjective to each individual beholder, it should always be most beautifully beheld by its creator, for only he or she knows exactly why and for what it was created.

And so, in this awareness, I will celebrate my ability to create beauty within the depths of my love. And I will allow myself to feel every part of what the ground and sky have to offer me, as I exist temporarily between the two, creating a body-soul experience that has felt all of life and is ready to leave when it must. And when it does, I will move into the next realm peacefully, knowing that with each passing moment I created art within and around this clay-made body in order to leave a piece of beauty behind on the earth for her eternal healing.

Because everything is healing. Everything is art. Everything is eternity. Everything is a single moment.

WAKING UP: A MOMENT OF CLARITY

DALE RYAN

With a brief prayer of gratitude for Bill (which is not his real name,) who chose a door-knob as his Higher Power and got a thirty-day chip at the first AA meeting I attended in the winter of 1983 in Minneapolis, Minnesota.

In 1983, I was in seminary studying to become a pastor. Ministry was a second career for me. Prior to going to seminary, I had earned my PhD in biochemistry and taught at the University of Wisconsin, Madison. It became clear fairly early in that career, however, that it was not going to be my final destination. I was called to ministry, so I went to seminary. When I started seminary I had done no work on any of my "issues." (*Issues? Not sure what you're talking about.*) I was just a good Christian, committed, faithful, doing the right things—"No problem here." I was going to learn how to be helpful to all the other people who so desperately needed assistance with *their* issues.

The first AA group I attended was to fulfill the requirements for a class in pastoral care. I went because I wanted to get a good grade in the class. I remember a bit about that semester. I had just completed a lengthy paper on the Christology of Maximus the Confessor. Maximus was a theologian and monk who was tried as a heretic in 658 because he refused to accept the monothelite views which were favored by the emperor at that time in Constantinople. My paper was very thoughtful. Full of serious, multi-syllabic words in several languages. Deep. I remember thinking that I was really into advanced Christian stuff. Now that I think about it, actually, the *"advanced Christian stuff"* was exactly what I was hoping to acquire in seminary. I wasn't all that interested in the introductory Christian stuff.

So, as you may have guessed by now, I arrived at my first AA meeting with a fairly significant deficit in the spiritual humility department. I don't think spiritual humility was much of a priority for me at the time. I wanted to know all the right answers to all the right questions. I wanted to be smart enough, competent enough, gifted enough, and whatever enough to be a really good pastor. That's not the kind of goal that a person with even a modicum of spiritual humility is likely to pursue.

I arrived at my first AA meeting early and with a bad attitude. I didn't know how this could possibly be helpful to me in my goal of becoming an advanced Christian. The meeting was in the basement of a downtown building that had seen better days. There were cheap folding chairs in a circle and coffee brewing on a folding table off to the side. I sat down on one of the chairs. It became obvious to me (almost immediately) that this was not going to be a meeting for Betty Ford graduates. It was a street drunk meeting: pretty hard-core, down-and-almost-out alkies, and lots of homeless folks.

Because I arrived early, I had some time to think (and be anxious) before the meeting started. I remember distracting myself by mentally reviewing my arguments about monothelite Christology in the paper about Maximus. I remember feeling good about the work I had done, and I remember thinking (even as I write this thirty years later, it's still embarrassing!): *I went to seminary to learn about God. And I'm pretty sure that I already know more about God than anybody who is going to show up in this room. So what am I doing here?*

The only thing I remember about the meeting is a guy who I will call Bill. Bill got a thirty-day chip that night. He was pretty scruffy looking. The streets had taken their toll. But he had been sober for thirty days. When he came forward to pick up his thirty-day chip, he was given the opportunity to speak for two minutes.

I don't remember exactly what Bill said. He was not an accomplished public speaker. He wasn't very clear. But he said something like: *My best thinking stole the last thirty years of my life. Can't say I understand it, but seems like something's changed. I couldn't figure out what to choose as my Higher Power, so I chose a doorknob. And I've been sober now for thirty days. Go figure. I'm a grateful drunk.*

There was actually more information in Bill's body language and non-verbal cues than in his words. It was obvious that this was a man who had *experienced* something. He might not have known the word "grace," but that's what I saw. I saw a man who had experienced grace for the first time in his life.

He was radiant with it. Overflowing with it. Hopeful. Eager for more.

Before going on, I should probably say a word about the "doorknob" part of the story. If you are in AA or any other twelve-step fellowship, you probably already get this. But it's pretty confusing to other people. It just sounds completely crazy. So let me be clear: nobody, absolutely nobody, really thinks that a doorknob is a very good choice for a Higher Power. It's a kind of an inside joke. It's what you say when you are completely clueless and know that you are completely clueless. Roughly translated it means: *I haven't got the slightest idea who or what might be available to help me, but I've completely come to the end of self-reliance. I can't do this. So if there is a Higher Power who is willing to restore me to sanity, I'm available to be helped.* I know that may not sound like a whole lot of faith to some people. But it was enough faith to turn Bill's life upside down. It was his mustard seed of faith. The smallest amount imaginable.

Thankfully, God was paying attention and didn't insist that Bill produce a larger quantity of faith before coming close and doing what needed to be done.

It was obvious to me that Bill had experienced something remarkable. He had not been able to string together more than a couple of days of sobriety in thirty years, but that day he was thirty days sober. And he knew—with absolutely certainty—that he was not the one who had made that happen. His sobriety was something he had received, not something he had accomplished. He had experienced grace. Raw, undeniable, miraculous, knock-your-socks-off, unbelievable grace. He didn't have many words for it yet. But he had the thing to which those words refer. He was at the beginning of a spiritual awakening, and it obviously felt good.

I don't think I paid any attention after Bill sat down. I don't remember anything else about that meeting. I do remember sitting there with a very strange emerging awareness. It first arose as a question: *How can it be that Bill, who knows absolutely nothing about God, can be having such a*

powerful and grace-full experience of God while I, a person definitely into the
advanced Christian kind of stuff, am so completely miserable?

You see, at that time in my life I had precious little experience with grace of the kind Bill was experiencing. I knew, of course, all about grace. I had all the words that Bill didn't yet know. Big multi-syllabic words. I knew the subtleties, the complexities, the nuances, the disputes. I could have written a very nice advanced Christian essay about the fine points of the Doctrine of Grace. But there was nothing in my life to compare with the experience that Bill was living.

Nothing.

Looking back, it is quite clear to me that there was a dissonance, a gap, between the God of my formal theology—the God which appeared in my "statement of faith"—and the god who I actually lived with—the god who I woke up to in the morning, the god who shaped my daily life. It is possible to have a thoroughly orthodox formal theology, the kind that would get you an "A" on a theology exam in seminary or Bible school, and yet actually worship and serve a very different kind of deity. It is possible to get grace right in theory and still be driven relentlessly by the need to get everything right because the god we actually worship and serve is very different from the deity of our formal convictions.

From an early age I have had the kinds of ideas about God that most Christians would find perfectly acceptable. But the deity I actually served for most of my life, my actual Higher Power, was what I call the god-of-impossible-expectations. This god is the kind of stern-faced, unapproachable deity who has little to say beyond: *You should try harder,* or, *That's not good enough.* This impossible-to-please deity was an idol that I had crafted for myself primarily out of my experiences in childhood.

The god-of-impossible-expectations, it turns out, is a worse choice for a Higher Power than a doorknob. Much worse. Firstly, a doorknob doesn't constantly yell at you, nor does it spend all day writing down every mistake you make, every impure thought, every shortcoming. And secondly, a doorknob has the distinct advantage of not being "me." It is at least outside of me. Other than me. But the god-of-impossible-expectations, like many other gods who are not God, was entirely a psychological construct created by me, owned by me, and in residence deep within me. Its main job appears to have been the distribution of shame and fear. And it seemed to have an infinite supply of shame and fear to distribute. It was the voice which drove my relentless quest to get everything right, to have all the right answers to all the right questions, to be without fault. This deity did not distribute grace. It was too busy reminding me of how undeserving I was to receive any of it.

Sitting in that room, mid-winter in Minneapolis, as Bill's words rattled around in my obsessional brain, something became clear. I awoke to something. It was the first of a series of moments-of-clarity that changed my life. Moments of clarity are almost always difficult to explain. I can't fully explain this one. The best I can do is to say that I "heard" something like this: *If you are not able to somehow find the spiritual humility to learn from Bill, you will be doomed to a life of trying—trying harder and trying your hardest to please an impossible-to-please god.*

All I can say is that the plain, simple truth was that a guy who had chosen a doorknob as his Higher Power had something that I knew I needed. Desperately needed. It was something about spiritual humility, something about the futility of self-reliance, something about letting God be God.

My idolatrous attachment to the god-of-impossible-expectations was not miraculously removed that day. It took a long time to throw that bum out, to clean house. But it probably also took quite a while for Bill's sobriety to become stable. We both needed a one-day-at-a-time experience of grace. And that, thankfully, is exactly what was available to both of us when we got out of the way.

Dear God,
Thank You for Bill.
Thank You for sending him to that meeting.
Thank You for having him say what I needed to hear.
Thank You for helping Bill stay sober when he didn't know anything about You.
     When he was blind, You led him down unfamiliar paths.
Thank You for helping me when I thought I knew everything about You.
     When I was blind, You led me down unfamiliar paths.
Both of us, in our blindness, needed You desperately.
And there You were.
You woke us up.
I am still one-day-at-a-time grateful.
Amen.

RE-ALIGNED AGAIN

KELLY HALL

I ran from life for a lifetime, it seems. Found ways to deny both positive and negative aspects of my humanity, I suppose just to survive. Which made me a survivor. Yes, to that I completely agree: I was a survivor. In 2004, in the height of striving to overcome (and when I say overcome, I mean to defeat the constant barrage of self-loathing, the fear of failure, and self-imposed pressure to be nearly perfect at being a wife, mother, daughter, sister, friend, and earth-bound citizen), I accomplished my greatest fear (failing of all the aforementioned tasks) and fell into depressed times. The best description I could give would be to tell you that I was full of water, but not drowning. Imagine containing the unheard cries and tears of ages, the ones that just would not release and be healed, hurting and feeling numbed out from the fullness all at the same time. Immobile. Dramatic, I know, everything was very real drama. Face in the couch, hair an unwashed mess, thinking unceasingly, yet unable to communicate anything clearly.

This is where God found me, clinging to my things (expectations, judgments, shames, and consequences) and the reality I had bought into. I walked into a community that allowed me to sit, listen, and absorb such insanities of grace, love, and freedom. In this place, I began to find words to tell of where I had been and the hope of where I am going. The writing that came first portrayed a woman severely disconnected to any sensation of being human, or alive at all. It was awkward and unwelcoming, and still operating in the striving system I was driven to write something people would be moved to read.

Over time, God invited me into a new creation—one that was not about performing or accolades, but about healing. Don't get me wrong; walking into a church was not a cure-all for my depression. Medication, therapy, art, and open-ended conversations with my Creator became my modalities. Writing, then, became a working confession, a meditative time of revelation of all that I have denied—including gifts—both personally and communally. He is teaching me to gather words that both heal me internally and speak wholeness over the groanings of the greater community. Healing is for all, after all. We can all survive, that is certain. We have the tools we need to get by and maybe even to look like we are doing much better than we are. I believe, though, that we were meant to thrive, to burst with the same energy that vibrates a seed to sprout, to wiggle and birth through the soil to the sun, and to express that striving, that energy, the collective love and its resulting freedom. I want to be a *thriver*.

For all times, for this space, this opportunity to create with friends for the greater body, I am forever grateful to God, my loving source of inspiration.

I rejected my worth,
denied the truth from Whom I am birthed,
became a brick & played my part,
unstable from the start, hardened to the heart—
I can't hold up this world on my own
even the mortar's crumbled undone,
and the home I existed in the past—
the place I thought was built to last—
turns out to be an aching wound
from the way I've gained and assumed.

So, Water, fall—let these tears be my call
Lord don't hold back, take it all,
take it all.
In all relations now and past,
breathe to life what's meant to last
may the consequences of then and now,
heal beneath the salve of Your know-how
and love become the remedy,
the power of God that sets us free
because grace is not wisdom's fool,
a dying art, a jester's tool—
it comes as tender to the flame
Spirited passion of the Holy Name.

I have to still and just rest in it,
agree to the places of Your benefit,
and remember the cause to which I claim
leveled the bricks and aligned them again,
to befriend the rich to the poor
so comfort is a luxury no more,
but the constant of kingdom living
and the inspiration of all giving.

See this poem come to life at: THEWORKOFTHEPEOPLE.COM / REALIGNED-AGAIN

THIS MORNING

for Uncle Steve

KELLY HALL

God sent for me this morning,
blew the mouth of our house open wide
fluffing its cheeks and nudging me with life-saving air,
crisp and cool (as January is),
and I move enough to greet my Maker with a morning yawn,
releasing the staleness of my own dreams
to fall awe-full
at the threshold of inside-and-out
as He, pardon me, They, came winding
through, Spirit awakening the bells,
combing through the chimes,
conducting the hounds to key up
and wake the trees, reluctant like high-school boys
to do anything but flex and shoulder up to one another
growing used to their more manly stature
while still taking strength in numbers—
circling, bending, resisting, surrendering and fine-tuning
to both the familiar and yet an altogether new day
they shook birds free to fuss about from branch to branch,
oh the strength of limbs, I think, as I agree in my soul
to a continual communion,
becoming identified—known.
I threw off my cover and joined God in the middle of earth,
to end my fast of words in the clarity of morning:

You are, and I am alive . . .
Yes, me too.

CHILD OF GOD

JASON FLOYD

"How can someone be born when they are old? . . . Surely they cannot enter a second time into their mother's womb to be born!"

—*John 3:4*

Have you ever tried to have a conversation with someone who was asleep? Sat down comfortably beside their bed and asked them about their day? If you have, I am sure you realized all too soon that it was to little or no avail. It can be just as difficult when we set out to describe "waking up" in the spiritual context. Any such explanation will only be truly understood by those who have already awoken, perhaps like a mother trying to describe the pains of childbirth, or the love a mother has for her newborn, to an expectant mother. It is simply something she has to experience herself to fully grasp something other mothers understand completely.

Hope is not lost to sleepers, however, so should you find yourself at all intrigued by the mystery of "waking up," then hope awaits you. The alarm has sounded. Breakfast is ready. You have been called, and in due time you will awaken from your slumber to find a new heaven and a new earth—a world that no longer consumes you, or you it.

"*Behold, I am making all things new.*" —*Rev 21:5*, ESV

This awakening is sometimes referred to as entering into the mystery, though wrongly so, I think. When you arise into this new world it will be as if you left the mystery behind. Life will cease to be an endless torment of break-ups, lies, death, and addiction. You will begin to see clearly for the first time. In fact, it is the life you left behind that will become the mystery. It will seem to have been a dream, or perhaps more aptly a nightmare, but a nightmare that you no longer recount with fear or even regret. Every failed relationship will have been an arrow pointing the way. Every broken promise will have been a beacon leading you onward. Every person you've lost along the way will represent a helpful traveler giving direction. Every "never again" or "just this last time" will become a mile marker pressing you nearer. Upon arrival, life will cease to work against you. You will no longer be a victim of anyone or anything. You will see that you were merely in a deep slumber, inhaling toxic fumes as the house slowly burned. There will be no regret. Nothing will have been wasted.

Oh, you'll be groggy for sure, disoriented as you awaken from such a long, restless dream. At first the dream will seem so real. You won't trust your awakened state, but as you begin to encounter the characters in your dream, you'll see that they aren't real. You can touch them and talk to them, but they survive on a different plane than you. They are sleepwalking. You'll want to wake them and invite them to join you, but you can't. It's not their time. You'll be okay with that. You will set out on a mission of discovery, clearing a path for their eventual journey. When they are ready, you will return for them.

While on your new mission, you will find yourself wrestling with a supernatural desire to forgive the unforgiveable, to redeem the unredeemable, to love the unlovable—even yourself. Simple things that previously went unnoticed will exhilarate you. You will find yourself praising God for coffee, safety pins, and toilet paper. You'll see both the hopelessness and hope existing in others at that same time. Your captors will lose power over you. You will notice the chains that once bound you are now binding them and, perhaps even more peculiar, you will want to free them as well.

Things that alarm others and once alarmed you won't matter anymore. At first you might go through the motions of your previous ways of acting out, but only because it will look and feel strange to be at peace. Then you'll remember that those around you are still asleep and, in time, you'll gain sufficient trust in your awakened state to begin to share your new reality, even with those who are still sleeping. More and more, you will allow your radiance to shine. Many of those closest to you will be quite uncomfortable with this new you. Your light will expose the darkness within them. It will threaten the constructs of their ego-based slumber. It will scare them. After all, light has no boundaries, nor is it containable.

Your light will be the Light of the living Christ, and wherever it shines, it will produce the call of the living Christ. His authority will rest in you. The call of Christ can be an unsettling, if not terrifying, interruption to the ego-centered life. Things are about to change. The walls that have held you in will begin to crumble. All that you have depended upon in the past will become of little use to you now. You'll still have your family, your friends, your hobbies, and your job. You may even retain your less popular addictions for a while, but they will no longer define you. They will no longer own you. You will be free.

When you wake up, you'll also find you are no longer at home. Perhaps you'll awaken in the same house and town where you've always lived, but you'll sense they are only temporary and you are merely a traveler passing through. You will lose your attachment to them and all things of this world. You will still enjoy them, but things, as with people, will have little hold over you.

Your priorities will shift. The distractions that held such meaning for you will be replaced by the desire to build relationships both brief and lasting. This will matter most. You won't have time for it, but you will do it anyway, and somehow, supernaturally I suspect, your time will be returned to you. You will begin to realize, subtle though it may be, that you once used and manipulated people to meet your own needs. As your needs diminish, so will your desire to control and objectify others. You will see them for who they are to God and not for what they might offer you. You will no longer need them, so you'll be able to love them, truly love them, perhaps for the very first time.

"And now these three remain: faith, hope and love. But the greatest of these is love."   —*1 Cor 13:13,* NIV

Like an expectant mother poised for delivery, you will experience fear and pain in your awakening, oftentimes excruciating, but hope of the prize that awaits will see you through. You may wish to just let things be the way they are or have been in the past, but you know you cannot. Joy leads you onward. New life is being ushered into the world. That new life is you and all those that will heed your call as you move forward. This is what is meant by rebirth. There will be no second entry through your mother's womb. You will be both mother and child, solely embodying the agony, ecstasy, and reward. Once labor is complete, though, you realize He was nearby all along. The proud Father will emerge, and in His radiant presence, the newborn child of God.

"So then, let us not be like others, who are asleep, but let us be awake and sober."
—*1 Thessalonians 5:6,* NIV

AWAKENING AS PRAYER

JUANITA RYAN

"Awake, my soul!
Awake, harp and lyre!
I will awaken the dawn.
I will praise you, Lord, among the nations;
I will sing of you among the peoples.
For great is your love, reaching the heavens;
your faithfulness reaches the skies."

—*Psalm 57:8-10*

Prayer is awakening. We have a tendency to fall asleep spiritually. Too often we forget who we are and what life is about. We forget the deeper realities of our existence. We fall asleep.

Prayer wakes us up. The very act of prayer is an acknowledgment of our spiritual nature. It is an acknowledgment of our longing for relationship with God. It reminds us that there is more to life than what we see and touch. It reminds us that there is more to life than the pressures we face and the distractions we chase after. Prayer wakes us up to God's presence. It awakens us to the reality of the spiritual significance of ordinary life. It awakens us to the truth that life is an adventure to be lived in relationship with God.

But there is more. The awakening that prayer can bring has the potential of moving deeper and deeper into our hearts in a way that heals and frees us from the depths of our stupor and forgetfulness.

Many of us have forgotten who God is. We have forgotten that God is love and that God's love for us is intimate and unconditional. And many of us have forgotten who we are and who others are. We have forgotten that we are all God's beloved children.

We may have come to believe that the opposite is true. We may have come to believe that God is harsh, punitive, or abandoning. And we may have come to believe that we, or our neighbors, are unlovable. But this is not who God is. This is not who we are. And it is not who our neighbors are.

As we open our hearts and minds to God's loving Spirit, these lies about God, about ourselves, and about our neighbors can begin to fade. We can begin to awaken to the reality of who God is, who we are, and who our neighbor is.

In prayer, we are invited to awaken more and more to the reality of God's love and to awaken more and more to the reality that we, along with all others, are loved. This is an awakening in joy and freedom, to be our true selves, to honor the dignity of each human being, and to rest and rejoice in God's unfailing love for us. This is the deepest awakening of all.

Prayer is learning to sing with the psalmist, "Awake my soul! Awake, harp and lyre! I will awaken the dawn. I will praise you, Lord . . . for great is your love, reaching the heavens; your faithfulness reaches the skies."

Thank You, God, for waking me up.
Thank You that prayer invites us to the deepest awakening
        of all,
to remember who You are
who we are
and who our neighbor is.
Thank You for Your unfailing love.
Thank You that we are Your beloved children.
Your love is so great, so vast, so faithful!
Thank You for waking me from my fearful slumber
into the glorious truth of who You are.

PRAYER SUGGESTION:

Celebrate the awakenings that prayer has brought into your life. Ask God to show you what further awakenings He might have for you.

TASTES OF ENLIGHTENMENT

AARON EDWARDS

Waking up is very much like what alcoholics refer to as experiencing "a moment of clarity." It is when you suddenly grasp or understand something that was previously unclear or clouded. But it is more like something that you allow, not so much something you make happen. Some may even call this a revelation or epiphany. I believe this is what follows the experience of powerlessness and surrender. It's first realizing that there is something that you are asleep to, something you are not seeing.

When I find myself relying on patterns of thinking, or other various forms of addiction, in order to 'wake up,' I must first see that I am in some way numbing myself out of fear. I believe the fear is fear of scarcity, that somehow love is going to become depleted. Fear that God's resources are going to run out. Fear that I am not enough. Believing this causes me to want to 'sleep' through my life.

But this is a false reality. And when I have a conscious realization of what is not truth, I am preparing room for what is truth. The ultimate truth is that there is a constant, unending, always growing supply of God's love and grace. When I wake up to this truth, I am born again. I look around and can see God's love and grace in the most unlikely places, places I never would have seen previously.

Ultimately, waking up is seeing a truth that we previously chose not to see. It starts with the truth about why we have chosen to sabotage ourselves. It ends with a much more profound truth—the truth of who we really are in Christ—and only then can we look at our own addictions without self-condemnation. We eventually see that nothing on our crooked path was ever wasted. The healing love of Christ comes pouring in, and we get a true taste of enlightenment.

CONNECTING OUR SOUL TO THE SONG

SETH WOODS

Five years ago, at the break of Easter Sunday morning, I drove to meet a new friend at Cisco's on East Sixth Street of Austin, Texas. I did not know it yet, but this person would change my life—where I lived, how I thought, how I spoke, and how I saw the world, others, and myself. It was the beginning of the end, and the end of the beginning, or something along those lines.

My new friend was visiting from another state. As I drove to her sister's house to pick her up for our sunrise breakfast, I was brimming with excitement about this wonderful new friend and about taking her to a sweet breakfast joint, but also excited in large part because I was listening to the brand new Bill Callahan record: *Sometimes I Wish We Were An Eagle*. The day was shaping up to be one of my most memorable Easters: breakfast with a new secret crush at sun-up and a new record from a trusted and beloved artist for the ride. Huzzah!

There was something about that time, that person, and those songs. There was a swirling around them—not the nauseous kind you get at the end of the party, more like the mystical, enchanted kind. Of course, the thing about enchantments is that there are "good" ones, and there are "bad" ones, and most of the time you can't ever tell them apart until it's too late. Or, you know, ever.

Fred introduced me to my new friend just a few weeks earlier. I had a fairly long beard at the time, and Fred had given me a nickname because of it. "Oh, Holy Prophet," he called to me from across a semi-crowded room, "I want to introduce you to someone."

"Hi, Holy Prophet," she said as she took my hand. "I'm the

Harbinger of Doom."

Yep. Enchantments.

Sometimes I Wish We Were An Eagle struck me from the first chord. The swirling I had felt in the air during that whole spring formed into arpeggios, fit into melodies, and was clothed in lines of lyric.

> *"Something too big to be seen*
> *was passing over and over me."*

It was one of those records, one of those experiences of recorded music that felt separate from its creator, from the historical context it had come from.

Okervil River's *Black Sheep Boy* had been that for me, along with Crooked Finger's *Dignity And Shame*. Both records came into my life after my first major heartbreak in my early twenties, and I listened to them front to back day after day while trying to understand how these bands had been able to write an album about my life—my heart and soul—in that very season. "Prophetic," was the word I would murmur to myself, only half joking while sort of nervously looking over my shoulder to see if anyone was rolling their eyes or shuffling off their fleshly disguise for something a little more angelic.

It felt like it was either a cosmic, mean-spirited joke, or the beginning of a magic realism novel come to life, because it was as if, all of the sudden, Will Sheff and Eric Bachman were going to walk off the street, sit down in a booth at the shitty diner where I washed dishes, and tell me the grand reason I had been chosen for the pain I was feeling, all over a cup of coffee and chocolate chip pancakes.

Sometimes I Wish was a similar type of record. But instead of telling me about what I already knew was going on in my life, it spoke to me of things less familiar—the feeling of direct communication from the songs was the same. I knew there was a message hidden there for me, and me alone. I just couldn't figure out what it was.

Callahan's music had been important to me before. As a songwriter, he had challenged me on the form a song can take, on repetition of lyrical and musical phrases, and on alternate takes on narrative. "What can a story be?" was a growing question in my fledgling creative brain. The songs on *A River Ain't Too Much To Love*, his last record under the name Smog, had an almost Astral Weeksish spirit about them. I wouldn't have been surprised to hear him flow from, "Let me see the colts/that will run next year," into a string of, "Say goodbye to Madame Georges," or, "The love that loves to love the love that loves the loves." That was my first introduction to any of his music, and it was very much a case of being at the right place in the right time for me. I was sold, even on the more awkward, earlier Smog records.

As I began my relationship with this new record, I could tell there was something different than other Smog/Bill Callahan records. And it felt appropriate, because I felt that there was something vastly different about this woman and this budding relationship than the others I had known. I felt that, once again, an album was speaking to me about what was going on in my life. *But what was it saying?*

To tell the truth, it was saying some things that were still pretty uncomfortable for me to hear. "It's time to put God away," was something that I did NOT want to hear. I worked as the music pastor for a small church in Austin, and my job and community were dependent on me keeping God decidedly un-put-away! "This is the end of faith/no more must I strive/to find my peace/to find my peace in a lie." Sounds awful and unknown and terrifying. Nope. No, thank you. I'm fine with skipping that incredible last track to this prophetic record. Thanks very much, have a nice day, come and see us again.

The thing I *didn't* want to hear in those lyrics wasn't some vision of my life to come. What made me uncomfortable was the way the singer was able to get insight on me right then and there, assess the situation, and then continue to tell me all about current life—regardless of how many avoidance tactics I tried.

But isn't that the thing about true prophecy? It's not about predicting the future, or telling us what is going to happen, when and how. Prophecy speaks to today, to the moment at hand.

"Woe unto thee!" says the prophet. "Hey you! Yeah, you, over there by the bar with the trucker hat on. Yeah. You got some shit going on, man. I can see it all over your face. I'm not talking about how you'll die someday, dude. I'm trying to tell you about what is killing you right now. So listen up, 'cus this next one's for you, you poor bastard."

Prophecy is the wake up call in the gut of your soul. It's that voice, as David Bazan sings, "That still, small voice/begging you to shut the f@$! up."

In a radio interview for his latest album [1] with the Bad Seeds, Nick Cave was asked about how his song writing was moving away from a narrative form to a more abstract form. "They're still narrative songs," he argued:

> I write narratively. I'm a very visual person. It's all about . . . every life is about seeing for me. I can't write a song that I can't see, so I don't actually write in a more abstract way than what rock-and-roll is generally written about, which are these expressions of the heart, you know, "Woah baby, I love you," and all that sort of stuff. I feel it very difficult to write like that. . . . These songs are narrative in the sense that it becomes a kind of tyranny of the narrative, because the listener always has to follow a story. Every time they listen to a song they have to follow this story, and I find that I've been for a long time trying to get away from that. So [my songs] are narrative songs but they're so abstracted that the idea of following the story is kind of futile. They're much more about entering into a world, an atmospheric world.

When the listener hears a man crooning about finding his thrill "on blueberry hill," the world they are invited into is a very closed and specific one. It doesn't take much imagining to wonder what specific thrill, exactly, is happening on said hill. On the other hand, we have this scene: "She lay beside me like a branch from a tender willow tree/I was as still, as still as a river could be/when a rococo zephyr/swept over her and me." This scene is far more ambiguous, giving the listener question after question, and answering few of them. "Well maybe this was all/all but meant to be/maybe this is all/is all that meant to be." The head

---

1   SEE HTTP://YOUTU.BE/0PIDB53LQKE, ACCESSED 2/2/2015

no longer knows, but the heart hears and understands. This is the way of the poet and prophet.

Joseph Campbell spoke of mythology in the same way:

A living mythology is a composition of mythological symbols, and a living mythological symbol is an energy-evoking and directing sign. A symbol of this kind, when it is functioning, evokes energy immediately. It hits you as music that you respond to, as a picture that you respond to, as a face that you respond to. It does not pass through the brain in order to bring about its response. The interpretation of symbols is then a secondary matter. The symbol works of itself directly, immediately, touching a releasing mechanism in the psyche. The source of these symbols is psychological. Each of us is limited in his own way. Each of us is capable of experiences that are his own, and differ this way and that from someone else's experience. And now, when a mythological image is presented to you in a rite, you should be allowed to experience it in your way.

My point is this: a ritual is an opportunity to participate in a myth. You are in one way or another, putting your consciousness, even the action of your body, into play in relation to a mythological theme. By participating in a ritual occasion, you are in a magical field, a field that is putting you in touch with your own great depth. And then to have someone come along with an interpretation of that ritual that does not correspond to your experience of it, you are being cut off from the symbolic experience. My point here is that the function of the church is best served when it gives people occasions and opportunities to participate in these great, eternal, mythical experiences without telling them how to experience it, without telling what the meaning must be. What I'm saying is that the rites work, but the dogmas don't.

Whoa baby, I love you.

Song is symbol, and the prophetic song is a living symbol. It short-circuits the brain long enough to kick you in the balls, to get the attention of your soul. Those drop-you-to-your-knees lines are rarely merely clever. They are doorways. They are questions. Or better yet, they are statements that produce questions in the listener, questions in your heart, before your head can even lip-sync the words to itself. "I Want to Hold Your Hand" is a fine piece of pop music, truly top notch. And getting your Easter Sunday clothes on and singing "Nothing But the Blood of Jesus" with the congregation is a nice, classic slice of religion. But these do not stir the soul so much as affix it in cement right where it stands. But to gather with your brothers and sisters, to seek for something unknown but glimpsed, to sing softly, "Be thou my vision, O Lord of my heart, naught be all else to me save that Thou art"—this is not a great statement of faith, but the murmuring of the Spirit, the breath that whispers, "You live, child," without spoiling the surprise of what you're alive for. This is that young man questioning: "Could you find me? Would you kiss-uh my eyes? To lay me down in silence easy, to be born again."

Cave continues:

> The narrative song can very often take away the kind of sense of discovery from the listener. When you listen to a song, you want to feel like it's your song, like you discovered it. That's what makes a great song a great song, is that you feel, as a listener, connected to that song. It's your song. You discovered it. You know more about that song than everybody else. It's speaking to you more than it's speaking to anybody else. That's what makes a great song. And in a narrative song, you feel that the story's already been told, and you don't feel that same kind of connection of the soul to the song.

I arose to Easter again this year, five years since that breakfast, five years since my life began to change so drastically, five years since I first heard that record. This morning as I made breakfast on my own, and washed the dishes in my small kitchen in the south valley of Albuquerque, New

Mexico, I put *Sometimes I Wish We Were An Eagle* on the turntable. I hadn't listened to it all the way through in quite a while.

Once again I am amazed how true that record rings for me now. To be honest, it's still hard for my sweet little wide-eyed Baptist boy soul not to believe that Jesus Christ didn't reach down and touch the hand of Mr. Callahan as he penned these songs, whispering, "There's a young man who's gonna need to hear what you have to say, Bill. You ready? Well, write this down." There's a fine line between magic realism and religious fervor sometimes. There's also a fine line between metaphor and reality. Just because Jesus didn't tell Bill Callahan to write those songs for me doesn't mean that those songs weren't written for me, or that Jesus didn't have a hand in it, whether either of them knew it or not. (They didn't.)

And here's what I heard, both five years ago, and today:

I started out in search of ordinary things. I started telling the story without knowing the end. Now I'm not saying we are cut from the same tree. But like two pieces of the gallows, we share a common dream. It seemed like a routine case at first. With the death of the shadow came a lightness of verse. I used to be darker, then I got lighter, then I got dark again. I started running, and the concrete turned to sand. I started running, and things didn't pan out as planned. Somewhere between the wind and the dove lies all I sought from you. I dreamed it was a dream that you were gone. I woke up feeling so ripped by reality. Love is the king of the beasts, and when it gets hungry it must kill to eat. One last black bird without a place to be, turns around in hopes to find the place it last knew rest. I fell back asleep sometime later on and I dreamed the perfect song. It held all the answers, like hands laid on. In case things go poorly and I not return, remember the good things I have done. Maybe this was all, all but meant to be. Maybe this is all, is all that meant to be.

I put God away. I ended up in search of ordinary things.

Five years later. The relationship is gone. Fred is gone. The church in

Austin is gone. The person I was then? Gone. I'm afraid that Cisco's might be gone too, although I don't know for sure. But that record remains. And those other people and places and times remain in it. For me, *Sometimes I Wish We Were An Eagle* is as synonymous with Easter morning as Santa is with Christmas. And it is because these songs are able to tell not just their own story, not just the story of their author, but my story as well. We need poets, songwriters, playwrights, and screenwriters, to tell us our story when we can't tell it ourselves—maybe even when we can. The reason we need prophets to connect our souls to their songs is that we need a song to connect our soul to.

"I used to be sorta blind. Now I can sorta see."

TATTERED DREAMS
PHUC LUU

My dreams, blurred lines, tattered edges
Between worlds, this one and the next
A steady interstate—where the scenery is always the same
Often wondering where I am
And confused upon immediate awaking
To this place or that

But I find ground in a familiar smile
Or the gentle touch
A voice that I recall,
A sound that brings me back
To His world, and these people
Place of difficulty and sometimes despair,
But also land of joy and completion
That no dream can capture
Or to which I find escape

When I return to this home, the here
Then my dreams betray me
They speak to me no longer
Words foreign
And I forget the siren's call
For I have already reached my shore

AWAKENING
THROUGH REST

TERESA McBEAN

"A being is free only when it can determine and limit its activity."

—*Karl Barth*

"Remember the Sabbath day by keeping it holy. Six days you shall labor and do all your work, but the seventh day is a sabbath of the Lord your God On it you shall not do any work, neither you, nor your son or daughter, nor your male or female servant, nor your animals, nor any foreigner residing in your towns. For in six days the Lord made the heavens and earth, and sea, and all that is in them, and he rested on the seventh day. Therefore the Lord blessed the Sabbath day and made it holy."

—*Exodus 20:8-11*

I am almost old enough to remember boredom. In the South, back in the day, every kid was bored on Sunday. The community shut down, even the gas stations. (Can you imagine planning long trips around the Sabbath?) I let boredom slip away decades ago and replaced it with his little friend, "tired." Of course, I didn't understand any of this until I began my own Sabbath practice, and maybe that's the point of waking up: there's a lot you don't notice when you're spiritually sleepy! When I lost boredom as my faithful companion and teacher, I diminished my bandwidth for noticing the holy and profound.

My eighty-plus-year-old father is not tired. Last weekend he left his home in Atlanta, Georgia on his Gold Wing motorcycle and drove seven hours to Myrtle Beach, South Carolina for a bikers' weekend. My father, coming to faith later in life, has learned how to embrace the Sabbath.

My father isn't much of a sermonizer. When you wait until you're almost seventy years old to go to church, you have fewer opportunities to be ruined by the sermons. However, I have found God using him to wake me, his pastor-daughter, up. This, I suspect, will be the greatest gift my father ever gives me.

Of course he went to church growing up—he is from the Old South! But at home, it was hard to find holiness. Once he began making his own rules, he left church behind, and I cannot judge him for this. He's a brilliant man, and I imagine he was an intuitive and alert child. How could he make sense of the Sabbath practiced in a home of favoritism, infidelity, and bitterness? During my childhood years, my father lived a congruent life. No Sabbath. No rest. No mention of holiness. The father I grew up with was successful. And then, one day, he no longer cared about success, and that's when life got interesting.

I didn't get a fancy job and go to work via private jet. I didn't acquire airplanes and a lot of cool motorized toys. I am not overly fond of country clubs and golfing. I've never built an airplane in my garage. I don't know how to write messages in the sky. (All of this and more my father has done.) Superficially, my dad and I are NOTHING ALIKE.

But I am productive, for God's sake. (Read that sentence with a tinge of sarcasm and you've caught my meaning.) And at the end of the day, although we chose different venues that resulted in different strategic plans, I am in many ways my father's daughter—I get stuff done.

But productive is the enemy of the Sabbath, and it sure as heck is the antithesis of holiness, without which spiritual wakefulness is impossible. All those years without a Sabbath eventually resulted in my dad collapsing within himself. He and my mom retired early to Atlanta, Georgia, and for some unexplainable reason, they started attending church. One day, a couple years into this radically different life, my dad called me with an amazing story:

"T, last night I was getting ready for bed and asking the Lord to for-give me for my sins—you know it's a long list—I wasn't asleep, and, this wasn't a dream, but the Lord came to me in a vision . . . " (My dad goes on to describe Him in great detail, which I cannot repeat with accuracy, so I won't repeat it at all). "I was scared, I can tell you that. I tried to reach my hand out to Him . . . to apologize in person, but He reached His hand out first! He touched me on the chest and said, 'Bob, you're forgiven. Don't bring this up again.' He was so gentle, so kind. But I got the message. I'm not going to bother Him with my past anymore."

"Wow," I said, resenting almost immediately a private visit from Jesus to my dad when I was up here in Richmond, Virginia doing the Lord's work almost single-handedly! "What did Mom say?"

"Aw, she just told me she was tired and to stop all that talking."

I could feel him smiling. Forgiveness-received introduced my dad to holiness-practice and regular Sabbath. After all, he has nothing to atone for. Nothing else needs achieving. He's done, in a good way.

For decades I have observed my dad almost lose his life—his abun-dant, full, loving life—to toys and trinkets that never filled him with light. I watched my dad, once dead, become restored. My dad is still the man who drives me crazy. I love him, but I continue to strongly disagree with many of his worldviews and decisions. Jesus forgave him, but He didn't perform a lobotomy! But even the most productive daughter has eyes to see that something is different: *my father is free*. He believes in practicing the Sabbath and holiness even though he'll never exegete a passage of Scripture or discuss hermeneutics.

My own stubborn resistance to Sabbath has made me slow to catch on. But as I watch my father love my mother, who is in failing health, I find myself unwilling to continue on my own faith journey without stop-ping to practice Sabbath and receive holiness. I take a day of Sabbath. I don't hop on a Gold Wing, but I do dust off my motorized bicycle and take it for a spin in my neighborhood. When my son visits for a week, I cease my labors and sit on the patio with him. This is holy. I listen more than I talk, which is hard but necessary in order to practice Sabbath. I go for a run and try not to beat my fastest time. In fact, some days I dilly dally, taking pictures and stopping to look for a lost dog on behalf of a young man who may not have deserved the favor, but I did it anyway.

I am less tired. I am less productive. My Father—in every sense of the word—is waking me up to old ways of seeing that are new to me. My Fathers remind me that I have nothing to prove, no performance to deliver. But, by God, I am awake. And it is a gift.

"Therefore keep watch because you do not know when the owner of the house will come back—whether in the evening, or at midnight, or when the rooster crows, or at dawn. If he comes suddenly, do not let him find you sleeping. What I say to you, I say to everyone: 'Watch!'"

—*Mark 13:35-37*

VISIO DIVINA

SEEING WITH THE EYES OF THE HEART

JERRY WEBBER

Lectio Divina is a core practice in contemplative spiritual life. The Latin phrase means 'sacred reading,' or 'holy listening.' It refers to listening with the ear of our hearts. *Lectio Divina* is a reflective hearing or attentiveness characterized by openness to a sacred text. We listen with open hearts, not imposing our agenda on the text but waiting to attend to the ways God stirs us through the text. In *Lectio Divina*, we pray by listening and meditating.

As *Lectio Divina* refers to 'holy listening,' *Visio Divina* refers to 'holy seeing,' or 'sacred attention.' Just as we learn to listen or hear with our hearts, so we can learn to see or attend with our hearts.

In *Lectio Divina* we listen for words or phrases that stir our hearts. In *Visio Divina* we notice images in the visible world that stir our hearts. The movements of traditional *Lectio Divina* may be helpful for *Visio Divina*:

Visio: Looking, seeing, or noticing that which catches your attention or draws your gaze. As you notice what stirs you, or *glimmers* for you, simply hold the image in your heart. What element of the visual image draws your attention? To what do you feel drawn?

Meditatio: Meditating on what you see. 'Chew' on what you see by rolling the image around in your heart. Open yourself to what the lines, colors, or figures may be saying to you. Notice the possible connections—or intersections—between your real life and some element of what you see. In short, allow what you see to speak into your actual life. How does God's Spirit stir you through that image?

Oratio: Speaking back to God. Enter into dialogue with God around the image that is stirring you inwardly. Bring the visual image into your prayer. Ask God what it is trying to say to you. You might even engage in dialogue with the visual image itself. Talk to the artist, to the painting, or to a figure represented in the painting. Ask the color what it is saying to you. In dialogue, open yourself to a deeper connection between your real life and the visual image to which you are attending.

Contemplatio: Resting with the visual image you have seen. As you sit with it, open yourself to whatever else God wants to speak into you through the visual image.

In the context of paintings and graphic arts, you might use this guide to 'holy seeing' as you walk through a museum exhibit. These are merely suggestions offered as a way of moving through *Visio Divina*:

Visio: Walk leisurely through the gallery, exhibit, or museum. Take time before each painting to notice the colors, brush strokes, lines, and images in the painting. Be alert to the paintings that stir you inwardly. As you walk through the museum, make notes about which works seem to draw you.

After you have walked the entire exhibit or gallery, return to the paintings you noted previously. Take a bit more time before each one. Pause before the painting and notice the lines, colors, or images that draw you. Look at the painting from different angles.

You might ask yourself questions like: "Is there some part of the painting that draws my attention in a special way? Does some part of the art work stir me inwardly?" At this point, you don't have to know why you are stirred. Simply ask for the grace to notice *when* you are stirred. When a painting or some part of a painting stirs your heart, hold onto that aspect of the painting in order to explore what it says to you.

You will want to narrow your *Visio Divina* to one or two works of art. Once you have determined which works of art most stir you inwardly, return to them. If possible, you might want to sit or stand before the painting.

Meditatio: Bring into meditation that aspect of the painting that stirred your heart. Listen to what it is saying to you. What might God be saying to you through it?

In some way this painting has stirred your heart. In *Meditatio,* you want to open yourself to the connection between this painting and your real life. What is the connection—or point of intersection—between this painting and your life? Why would this painting—or this subject matter, or these colors—stir you right now?

Allow God to speak to you through the painting. Further, you may want to allow the painting, the colors, the subject matter, or even the artist to speak to you.

You may need to sit or stand before the painting for a while. Write what you hear in a journal. Even in the middle of the art gallery, create a space of solitude and silence within your heart. Listen.

Oratio: You have heard God speaking through the visual images. You may have heard the artist or the painting speak to you. Now bring the dialogue full circle. Speak to God, to the artist, or to the painting, and keep the conversation alive.

Ask questions of God about what might be the significance of the painting for you.

Ask questions of the artist about what he/she would like for you to notice in a particular color or image.

In *Oratio* we draw the visual image into our spoken prayer or into our mental prayer. This is our response to *Meditatio.* It may take place in the exhibition itself, or it may take place later in a period of reflection. *Oratio* may be a movement that includes journal writing, poetry writing, or creative expression. It is our response to the first movement of God toward us.

Contemplatio: Rest. Allow the movements of *Meditatio* and *Oratio* to continue the dialogue of prayer within you, apart from your conscious thinking about them. Rest as openly as you can. Invite God to instill the fruit of your prayer and meditation into your heart. It may be helpful to close your eyes and sit still in a quiet place.

These guidelines are not hard and fast. After practicing *Visio Divina* for a while, you will find a rhythm in which you move in and out of the four movements without thinking about them. It is more important that you learn to see with the eyes of your heart than that you attend scrupulously to these guidelines.

BECOMING FAMILIAR

ANDY GULLAHORN

Imagine that someone you love and trust blindfolded you and took you to an unfamiliar place. You can't see it, but they do their best to describe it for you. It is described as a place that has everything you will ever need to be happy and content. A place that is somehow stunningly beautiful both for its simplicity and its complexity. A place beyond your wildest dreams. Then it is time to finally take off the blindfold and see it for yourself. And you wake up.

What if you are waking up *to* a dream instead of *from* one?

I have recently started trying to identify all of the trees in my yard. I know nothing about identifying trees (that isn't completely true—I knew what a magnolia tree looked like), but I was inspired to learn more after I heard a friend say that the way to love something is to become familiar with it. I have lived here for eight years and the trees have just been, well, trees. But in this season of trying to learn names and familiarize myself with them, I find that my normal walks through the neighborhood have turned into grand adventures, looking at all of the other trees that I haven't 'met' yet. It is as if I have been sleepwalking through the neighborhood all this time and now I am actually starting to awaken to the world around me.

Now I can add identifying trees to the long list of habits I have tried adopting to help me keep my eyes open to reality. That list includes meeting with fellow travelers on a regular basis, sharing my story, listening to others share their stories, sitting in silence, putting my phone away, and simply being outside. It is no surprise that when I open my eyes to the world around me, I find that it is, by its very nature, beyond my wildest dreams. I find it is stunningly beautiful both for its simplicity and its complexity. I find it has everything I need to be content and happy (even if those aren't the *only* ways I might feel). And I find that everyday someone I love and trust takes that blindfold off for me so I can once again have a chance to wake up. [2]

·

---

2   Listen Andy's song "The Surface of Things" here:

HTTPS://DL.DROPBOXUSERCONTENT.COM/U/13922983/02%20THE%20SURFACE%20
OF%20THINGS.MP3

THE SURFACE OF THINGS

A SONG

ANDY GULLAHORN

When's the last time we looked each other in the eyes
Last time we dressed up for the ball
Last time we felt a raging jealousy inside
Or any raging feeling at all

When's the last time we forfeited the last word
Last time we didn't care who won
When's the last time we risked being rejected but alive
Instead of just comfortably numb

We have been scratching at the surface of things
When rivers run underneath

There's a whole world happening just under our breath
Covered by the slinging of mud
There's a pain that doesn't even have a name yet
An injury hemorrhaging blood

There's a fire still flickering from years ago
Unsure if it should comfort or burn
There's a hope that's hidden in the water below
Patiently waiting its turn

We have been scratching at the surface of things
When rivers run underneath

Put your ear to the ground
And your fist through the wall
Chase the rumbling sound
That says maybe we're not dead after all

It's not too late to start our hearts beating again
Not too late to **wake up to a dream**
Not too late to walk together to the water's edge
Kneel down and take a drink

We have been scratching at the surface of things
When rivers run underneath

"The hour has already come for you to wake up from your slumber, because our salvation is nearer now than when we first believed."

—*Romans 13:11*

"Blessed is the one who stays awake"

—*Revelation 16:15*

ANNEAL IN ME

MATT RUSSELL

As I understand it, transfiguration is at the very heart of the gospel. By transfiguration, I don't mean that we get out of the place we are in, places which are broken and disfigured situations. Transfiguration is not being raptured out of pain and suffering and put under some type of protective force field, ferried to the other side of the event unscathed. There is a type of spirituality that configures and conceives the gospel and spirituality in this way. Believing that life is a narrative that moves from left to right and upward and over, or is, as Richard Rohr would say, "One uninterrupted success story," is not an idea to be found in the gospel, and although this idea is deeply engrained in the American psyche, I don't think it is found in you and me when we drill down past the surface. But it is a powerful, seductive idea. Yet pain and suffering, tragedy and trauma are unalterable parts of our lives and are therefore deeply connected to our spiritual development and experiences. Because of this, the gospel continues to bring us to transfiguration. By transfiguration I mean this notion that **if you look at something clearly enough, with the eyes of the Spirit, if you can stay with the pain and the unexplainable long enough, if you can remain, then sometimes the very thing that you are seeing, while not ceasing to be itself, is transfigured.**

But to be transfigured, we have to learn to remain, to stay with it, to watch, to stay awake, to wake up and not be led off—these seem to be core imperatives in the gospel and central to our recovery. A dominant theme of Jesus when He talks about "the Kingdom" is that there is a new way of envisioning reality. There are ways of thinking and living that are in a sense "unskilled," leading to perpetual pain and suffering. And there are ways of living in our world that allow us to wake up and remain with life long enough that a transfiguration is possible. *Sometimes the very thing you are seeing, while not ceasing to be itself, is transfigured.*

This past year I have been introduced to the poetry of George Herbert. Herbert was an English poet and Anglican priest who gave up a career in politics to tend to a small parish as a priest. He was known for his unfailing love for his parishioners. One of his contemporaries described him as a "soul composed of harmonies." In a collection of poems, Herbert plays with the imagery of glass: "A man that looks on glass, / on it may stay his eye, / Or, if he pleaseth, through it pass, / and then the heav'n espy." Herbert is pointing to a dual reality: the glass, what is beyond the glass, and the capacity to see both visions at the same time, creating one reality. We can see both the object and what is beyond. Waking up is learning to attend to these two realities, to live in the reality of what is in front of us, but also to the mystery of what is beyond us.

Herbert also wrote a poem called "The Windows," where he redeems the word "stain." He doesn't use the word; he just redeems it. Because the only context where the word "stain" is not used with a negative connotation is in stained glass. It is a poem about the reality of our own frailty and this dual vision that is possible: "Lord, how can man preach thy eternall word? / He is a brittle crazie glasse: / Yet in thy temple thou dost him afford / This glorious and transcendent place, / to be a window, through thy grace."

Herbert uses these great words: "brittle" and "crazy." In the Middle Ages, making glass was an art. If you ever visit an ancient building, you will notice that the glass is wavy and lumpy, and looks as if it is melting. There is a trade-off in glass making. If you made the glass really thin and clear enough to see through, it would become *brittle* and could shatter easily. So it was better to have it *crazy*, a little bit waved, but thicker. Hebert is saying that normally glass is either brittle or crazy, but here, it's like he is saying, "Lord, I am both—I'm brittle and crazy. I am thin and frail and easily broken, and I am thick and lumpy and impenetrable." And that is humanity. That is the condition we all find ourselves in. We are brittle and crazy, we are thin and frail and not as strong as we think we are, and we are thick and impenetrable.

But the poet says, I can be a window: "But when thou dost anneal in glasse thy storie, / Making thy life to shine within . . . / / Doctrine and life, colours and light, in one / When they combine and mingle."

With Medieval glass, you did not just paint color on the glass. Coloring the glass was a whole process called *annealing*. This is a great word, annealing. To get the color in stained glass, you heat the glass up with hot, molten silicon. The coloring process took the glass almost back to liquid in a fierce heat. The annealing process refers to what happens to the glass after if has been brought through a critical temperature and begins to cool. It is here that the glassmakers would pour in the colors and stain the glass. The annealing process left the stained glass either brittle or crazy.

And Herbert is pointing to this spiritual reality, this invitation, this place of transfiguration where God's grace assumes our passions, character defects, faults, and brokenness, and anneals God's story in us. So there's some point at which we become a window of grace, not by being some pure, clear, beautiful thing, but by this annealing process where our colors and the colors of Christ's passion run together in the glass. Brittle and crazy as we are, we awaken to the beauty of God making all things new. Even our stains are redeemed and made beautiful.

So as people stay with us, linger with us, it is not that we get "more spiritual and less human," but that the very place of our humanity, while not ceasing to be what it is, is transformed into a window of God's grace and love, transfigured into a place where heaven and earth mingle. And it mingles in the brittle, crazy contours of our lives.

BENEDICTION

KELLY HALL

Bless us, O God,
Grace be unto my eyes, gentle
     as sleep is swept from their corners,
     as light is welcomed in, soft at first
     then crisp and clear.

Hold me in this moment, give me fully to now.
In Your presence is where my heart knows freedom,
and can be brave enough to be tender, break and come alive again.

Now is where I remember that I am enough,
and that You Are Always, which is more than enough.
Let me feast and fill on this moment, and for life's sake,
feel the impression of the Light for as long as I can,
accepting as much grace as I can
so as to give as much as I can.

Build Your "Always" into our every day,
wake me to the knowing that I am now and forever Yours.

CONTRIBUTOR INFORMATION

The National Association of Christian Recovery exists to provide faith-based communities a process of transformational recovery to aid people suffering with addiction, trauma, and abuse. NACR.ORG

The Work Of The People is an independent ecumenical platform that produces and publishes short films to stir imagination, spark discussion, and move people toward discovery and transformation. TWOTP.ORG

We are so thankful for our contributors:

Shellee Coley is a singer/songwriter/blogger based out of Conroe, Texas. She has just released her third studio project, "Songs Without Bridges," and is currently touring locally and regionally. Find out more about her music, tour dates, and other projects she is involved with at SHELLEECOLEY.COM.

Aaron Edwards is Pastor of Sondays Church and Executive President of Tomball Renewal Center in Tomball, Texas. You can see what Aaron is up to at TOMBALLRE-NEWALCENTER.ORG.

Kim Engelmann is the Senior Pastor at West Valley Presbyterian Church in Cupertino, California. She received her Master of Divinity from Princeton Seminary and her Doctor of Ministry in Pastoral Care from Boston University. She is married to Timothy and is mother to Christopher, Julie, and Jonathan.

Jason Floyd is a native Houstonian and the founder of Amerisource Funding, Inc. He also serves on the board of several other small businesses and ministry organizations. Having been kidnapped by Jesus in 2003 from a life of financial ease and material opportunity, he now wakes each morning to the pressing question, "Why me, Lord?" His fabulous wife of twenty years, Sophia, partners with him daily in an effort to not ruin their three precious and wonderfully spoiled children. Jason can be contacted at JFLOYD@AMERISOURCEFUNDING.COM.

Taylor Gahm is an artist, blogger, and comedian. Keep up with Taylor's thoughts here: TAYLORGAHM.COM, or go light yourself on fire and search for his TedxHouston Talk on YouTube.

Andy Gullahorn was born and raised in the rich musical climate of Austin, Texas and then went to College at Belmont University in Nashville to join the legions of songwriters in the country music scene. Since 2004, he has released three records: *Reinventing The Wheel* (2007), *The Law of Gravity* (2009), and *Christmas* (2010). You can read a full bio and anything you ever wanted to know about Andy at ANDYGULLAHORN.COM.

Kelly Hall is an artist, poet, editor, wife, and mother. You can get to know her better (when she remembers to write) on her blog at INFINITELYVAST@BLOGSPOT.COM, or by watching her blessings shared on TWOTP.COM.

Phuc Luu is a teacher of theology and philosophy. He has authored several articles, journals, and books on the topics of theology, philosophy, proofs for the existence of God, culture, and pastoral care. Phuc also enjoys painting, cooking, and spending time with his wife, Paula Nguyen Luu, and their two cats, Bebop and Roxy.

Teresa McBean is a Pastor at Northstar Community in Richmond, Virginia and Executive Director of the National Association for Christian Recovery. You can reach her at either NORTHSTARCOMMUNITY.COM or NACR.ORG.

Scott McBean proudly serves as Associate Pastor to Northstar Community in Richmond, Virginia. Visit Northstar's website at NORTHSTARCOMMUNITY.COM.

Kathy McDougall-Yeager is Pastor & Curator at Zeteo Houston Church, an affirming congregation. She chooses to show up daily to the places where God dwells in between us. You can find her at KATHYMCDOUGALL.COM.

Joel McKerrow is a writer, performance poet, and educator. For more inspiration go to JOELMCKERROW.COM.

Matthew Russell is a pastor, instigator, father, husband, and friend. His day job is Research Fellow in Theology and Community Development at Duke Divinity, where he is leading a new initiative in Houston, Texas. At night he wrangles three boys and a few pets.

Dale Ryan is Associate Professor of Recovery Ministry at Fuller Theological Seminary (FULLERINSTITUTE.ORG) and a member of the Board of the National Association for Christian Recovery (NACR.ORG).

James Ryan is a writer and a person in recovery. He is the editor of STEPSTUDY.ORG and the author of *Becoming Recovered* and its blog: BECOMINGRECOVERED.WORDPRESS. COM. He has his Masters in Theology from Boston University and a Masters in English from California State University Fullerton. He currently serves as program director of a 12-step retreat center in New Hampshire.

Juanita Ryan is an author and private practice therapist. You can see more of her writing at JUANITARYAN.COM.

Gregg Taylor is the pastor of Mercy Street, a community in Houston that creates a safe place for the hurting, the lost, and the seeking to experience the radical grace and welcome of God. You can read more about Mercy Street at MERCYSTREET.ORG.

Pieter Van Waarde is a photographer and poet. Check out his website at PIETVAN-WAARDE.COM or his Facebook page PIET'S PICS.

Jerry Webber is a husband, father, son, brother, and friend. He finds life by living as an explorer. He writes, teaches, and companions persons on the spiritual journey.

Vocationally, he leads and gives vision to The Center for Christian Spirituality, a ministry of Chapelwood United Methodist Church in Houston, Texas. His blog is "Only a Sojourner" at ONLYASOJOURNER.BLOGSPOT.COM.

Seth Woods traversed light through a fractal fiction engine to come to this universe in 1981. He's been trying to get home since about 1985 or so. Until then, he is living in Albuquerque, New Mexico, where he walks his dog and makes music as the Whiskey Priest. You can find out more about this creature at THEWHISKEYPRIEST.BANDCAMP.COM.

Made in the USA
Columbia, SC
06 October 2022

68980386R00098